SHORT RATIONS FROM PATRIOTS POINT VOLUNTEERS

THE STORY OF THE NAVAL AND MARITIME MUSEUM AND ITS VOLUNTEERS

THE VIETNAM EXPERIENCE

FROM THE AUTHOR/EXECUTIVE EDITOR OF

SHORT RATIONS FOR MARINES

MAJOR RALPH STONEY BATES, SR., USMC (RET)

Palmetto Publishing Group
Charleston, SC

SHORT RATIONS FROM PATRIOTS POINT VOLUNTEERS

First Edition

Printed in the United States

ISBN-13: 978-1-64111-392-2

ISBN-10: 1-64111-392-8

IN MEMORANDUM

★★★

THIS PUBLICATION IS DEDICATED TO PATRIOTS POINT VOLUNTEER CAPTAIN JOHN FLINN, USMC (RET) DECEASED:

PHOTO PROPERTY OF RAMONA FLINN

John lived with his wife, Ramona, in Mt. Pleasant. Together they had two children, four grandchildren, and four great-grandchildren. He joined the US Marine Corps in 1948 at the age of seventeen. After boot camp, he was stationed at Tsingtao, China, where he served for a few months, departing when the Republic of China capitulated to the Chinese communists. After some time in the United States, he returned to the Far East in time for the amphibious landing at Inchon, Korea during the Korean War. He spent virtually the rest of his first enlistment in Korea, leaving the Marines in 1952. After being a civilian for a couple of years, he re-enlisted in the Marine Corps, subsequently becoming an Explosive Ordinance Disposal (EOD) specialist.

Among many other assignments around the world, for over a year he served in Okinawa cleaning up explosive ordnance remaining from World War II. In 1965, he moved from the enlisted ranks to become a second lieutenant, a *Mustang* Officer (an enlisted person who becomes an officer), and shipped out to the war zone of Vietnam, where he served for a year. Later, after a two-year stint as commander of the US Naval EOD School, Practical Training Unit, he retired from the Marines as a captain in 1970.

He then started a second career serving with the US Secret Service in the Munitions Countermeasures Unit, providing technical support to the President and Vice President Protection Details. Seventeen years later, in 1987, after serving four presidents, many foreign VIPs, and traveling throughout the world, he retired as Chief of the Hazardous Materials Countermeasures Branch of the United States Secret Service.

He then formed a private consulting company on explosives and security-related issues, providing services to many major multinational corporations and government agencies. He assisted in the development of training programs for the US Department of State's Antiterrorism Assistance Program, which trained hundreds of police and military students from multiple third-world countries. In 2005, he was a member of New York City's Lower Manhattan (World Trade Center) Counter-Terrorism Advisory Team. He continued to consult whenever the opportunity would arise.

John became a Patriots Point volunteer in April 2008. He was also a leader in the local Marine Corps organization called the Low Country Leathernecks. John Flinn will be remembered as a person who gave of himself, unselfishly, with zeal and enthusiasm all his life.

John died on 12 June 2018. Semper Fi, John. Go with God.

TABLE OF CONTENTS

★★★

108

Chapter 10 – Claude Rountree served in the US Army. Claude was born in Charleston, SC. He graduated from The Citadel in 1971, and entered the US Army after graduation. His statement as a volunteer sums it up. *As I walk up to the 'Fighting Lady,' drive the cart, wherever and whenever it's my shift, all my troubles just lift away. It's a great place to be and to volunteer.* Claude returns to his roots and continues to serve others.

112

Chapter 11 – Ralph Stoney Bates was an active duty Marine for twenty-six years, a deputy sheriff for sixteen years, and an author for the last seven years. His various books and articles are described in this anthology. He is a contributing author, and the executive editor of this publication, which, when translated, means his wife, Lyn, did all the actual grunt-work on this anthology. Actually, she edits Stoney's writings. Stoney reiterates *I am merely a writer; my wife corrects and amplifies my writings to give depth and relevant meaning to my words.*

138

Chapter 12 – JoAnne Hann found her dream job right out of high school, with the FBI. Yes, that FBI, the Federal Bureau of Investigation. From that platform of life, she moved into other careers before retiring and volunteering at Patriots Point. Read this volunteer's unique story.

144

Chapter 13 – Robert Newman learned in one quick moment a lesson that would last a lifetime. If you are going to do something, then—do it right! He tells his story.

149

Chapter 14 – Dave Sowers was drawn into the Marine Corps largely through the shadow of his Marine father, a veteran of WW II. But, that was not enough to prepare him for day one, his first day at Parris Island.

FOREWORD

★★★

I have known Stoney Bates, a volunteer at Patriots Point Naval and Maritime museum, for several years. I know him to be a dedicated and knowledgeable volunteer who is also a retired Marine, a deputy sheriff, retired, and an author of several published books, plus the author of several articles contained in some professional magazines such as the *Marine Corps Gazette.* When he approached me about his desire to solicit, develop, complete, and publish an anthology of the men and women who volunteer here at the museum, I gladly accepted and approved his offer, and as of the copyright date on this publication, it should be noted that he has devoted long hours and considerable personal expenses, soliciting people to relate their individual stories, and developing those stories into publishable book format.

Knowing he already had a published anthology titled *Short Rations For Marines*, a well presented book of personal true stories about and by Marines and Fleet Marine Force Sailors from all eras including World War II, Korea, Vietnam, today's War on Terror and the years in between, boosted my interest in his offer. I found his first anthology to be an interesting and informative publication of not only war-front personal stories, but also many unique personal, sad, terrifying, and humorous human interest events reaching across time and space of generations of Americans.

Perhaps no writer is more gifted than he at soliciting and cajoling the many volunteers of this museum to relate their individual personal backgrounds and stories. He very expertly weaves their background stories into their day-to-day experiences at Patriots Point where they meet and interact with visitors from around the world and from virtually every state and territory of this great nation. Now, with this publication, the reader may share in those experiences. Eighteen months of labor and love has produced *Short Rations From Patriots Point Volunteers*, a valuable insight into this naval and maritime museum and many of its most important assets—its volunteers, without whom this great museum could not function.

Our volunteers are from every walk of life. Many are military veterans, most of whom did their required obligation, returned to their civilian world and became good patriotic citizens. They fairly represent a cross section of Americans. I know most of these volunteers personally. I admit to being more than a little surprised at how interesting their lives have been. What is not surprising is the realization that these people are the foundation of our great nation, and therefore, the story of their lives is worth telling.

It must be mentioned that one of the important goals of this museum is to educate our youth. Sadly, today many are not aware of the generations of other young men and women who either walked the decks of these warships, trod the snow of Korean hills, or the fields and paddies of Vietnam, or simply did their duty at the many far flung outposts around the world, discharging obligations to their country. They continued to cast away youthful ambitions and dreams by serving their country in times of need, times of peril, and in times when duty called. Oftentimes, a few months earlier they were the star quarterback of their high school football team, or they were out at a popular drive-in on a nervous date, and a few were being the class-clown in school, then—suddenly, patriotic duty called. They were all young civilians who were asked or volunteered to serve. It is one of our goals to have today's youth meet that youth of yesterday here at Patriots Point.

Stoney, thanks for compiling these important stories. It is also our desire to share these many experiences with the public through this anthology offered through our museum gift shop. Profits will return to the museum via the Yorktown Foundation. Enjoy these stories from and of our Patriots Point Volunteers.

Mac Burdette, Executive Director of Patriots Point
Colonel USAR (Retired)
Executive Director
Patriots Point Naval and Maritime Museum
December 2018

INTRODUCTION

★★★

THESE ARE THE PATRIOTS POINT NAVAL AND MARITIME MUSEUM VOLUNTEERS AND THEIR PLACES OF DUTY:

COMPILED BY: RALPH STONEY BATES, SR.
MAJOR USMC (RET)
EXECUTIVE EDITOR

EDITED BY: LINDA "LYN" GALE BATES

This is a small part of a continuous, never ending story spanning time and distance. These are true stories of a *place* and of a *people* at that place. These people are significant and unique because they have temporarily set aside their normal day-to-day tasks of maintaining a business, a job, a household, a livelihood, a hobby, or retirement-earned leisure hours to devote their time, experience, and their personal memories to a *calling*. Their individual *calling* is to inject their personal character, memories, and personality into a dialogue with other people who are the visitors to this unique place, allowing these visitors to garner a much more meaningful experience during their short visit here. Their presence and dialogue, while in contact with visitors, tends to bring two historically significant steel warships and a static display of a recreated United States military facility (a Vietnam War era fire support base) from a long ago war into becoming more than inert displays; instead, they become living symbols, or living memorials to generations of Americans. They become alive. These stories are from the hearts, minds, and memories of Patriots Point Volunteers.

Their individual methods of interaction with visitors may vary; however their collective goal is to assist in projecting a genuine feeling, a genuine emotion. Injecting their personal feelings often evokes a deeper meaning, a deeper understanding of these magnificent historical displays. To many, it is a vital *calling* for these individual volunteers. That is one of many reasons most have devoted their time and energy to their assigned routine.

The arriving visitors come from every State and territory of the Union, and from numerous foreign countries, and they are seemingly attracted to this location for many diverse reasons. Some are simply curious, some are perhaps coerced, a few are seemingly indifferent, and then, some of these visitors are compelled to be here. Like many of the volunteers, they embrace a deeper meaning. Within the ranks of these daily visitors are many United States military veterans who, in some cases, though they may be a first-time visitor, are actually returning to something that flares up from an earlier time, an old ember residing deep within begins to ignite. A growing number of these veterans are returning to a familiar place, with familiar sights and sounds conjuring emotions from their past. Some actually re-experience that past, through gestures, verbal discourse, and visible introspection, ever so briefly, right here. Frequently, volunteer and visitor alike find that they share a common bond here in these familiar surroundings, rekindling old experiences with new remembrances.

These stories will concentrate on volunteer workers, their personal stories, and their sometimes close connection to those visitors, especially the military veterans, who often share their stories and experiences of those times past while together in this unique setting at this place, Patriots Point.

★★★

Patriots Point on the coast of South Carolina is part of the old Hog Island landmass and forms a cape jutting out into Charleston Harbor, east of the city of Charleston, and south of US Highway 17 in Mt Pleasant, South Carolina. Today, it is amply named. Why the name Patriot? Simply put, the title Patriot is bestowed upon one who is a proud supporter of, and/or defender of, his or her country and its interest, or its way of life. Within part of the confines of Patriots Point is the Patriots Point Maritime and Naval Museum. This museum holds physical remembrances of several wars fought by patriotic Americans during the Twentieth Century. World War II, the Korean and Vietnam Wars are represented by the massive aircraft carrier USS *Yorktown*, CV 10, while the nearby destroyer USS *Laffey*, DD-724, represents World War II and the Korean War, and the uneasy peace between wars. They also hold the lingering dreams, memories, and remembrances of the men of those generations who served aboard those warships.

Interestingly, both ships are the second modern warships by the same name. Both, the original *Yorktown*, CV-5, and the original *Laffey*, DD-459, were sunk early during World War II. These two ships, home ported at Patriots Point, replaced those two sunken warships. *Laffey* was the second ship of the United States Navy to be named for Bartlett Laffey, a sailor during the Civil War who was a recipient of the Medal of Honor for his stand against attacking Confederate forces on 5 March 1864. *Yorktown*, CV-10 was the fourth navy ship at that time to bear the name. It was originally to be christened as *Bonhomme Richard*; however, renamed after *Yorktown*, CV-5 was sunk. In all, five navy warships bore the name *Yorktown*.

Near these two navy warships, on a two-and-a-half acre plot of land stands a metal Quonset–like hut displaying three larger than life military ribbon awards affixed above the entrance door. These ribbons are the National Defense Service Ribbon, the Vietnam Campaign Ribbon, and the Vietnam Service Ribbon. These ribbons represent military medals awarded to any and all servicemen/women who served in Vietnam, or otherwise participated in that war from the surrounding waters or military airfields sending airstrikes into Vietnam, or other areas directly supporting US forces in the Republic of Vietnam. This Quonset hut is the entrance into *The Vietnam Experience.* Emphasis on the word *experience!*

It is significant, and appropriate, that this maritime and naval museum display images, and project sounds, to conjure, and/or evoke some of the emotional feelings of the war in Vietnam. Why Vietnam? Well, for several reasons. One is because America does not want that war to become a second "forgotten war" as occurred to the veterans of the Korean War. Another is because many of the participants of the war in Vietnam were not welcomed home as a patriot should have been welcomed. Indeed, many Vietnam veterans were chastised for their service in Vietnam. And, then yet another reason, maritime/naval personnel of the Department of the Navy were in sizeable numbers, participants in that war, in the air, on land, and at sea.

The United States Navy (along with the US Army) participated in the Mobile Riverine Force, often called the Brown Water Navy, conducting combat operations within the interior waters of Vietnam. Navy Mobile Construction Battalions (Seabees) supported the Marines and Naval shore installations. The Naval Support Activity (NSA) Hospital at DaNang treated many wounded personnel, and the navy fleet of warships, support vessels, and hospital ships, off the coast of Vietnam, supported the land forces with direct naval gunfire, aircraft strikes, and life-saving medical services, as needed. And, they were frequently needed. United States Marines, part of the United States Navy Department, participated in direct combat with two divisions and an aircraft wing, plus their massive supporting elements. Much of the war in Vietnam was clearly a maritime operation.

Vietnam was a war, much like any war, with the exception of the reception its participants received as they returned home, and, not to be forgotten, the micro-management of combat operations by Washington bureaucrats and politicians. In a small way, *The Vietnam Experience* at Patriots Point tends to provide the casual visitor with a suggestive sense that those men and women who served their country over there deserved and still deserve a belated welcome home from that war. That lack of a welcome homecoming is one of the reasons Vietnam Veterans commonly greet each other with the expression "Welcome Home, Brother!"

As one enters from the back door of the Quonset hut to the outside exhibits in the two-and-a-half acre compound, the sounds of unique wildlife combined with the flap, flap, flap, or wop, wop, wop of rotor blades atop helicopters landing and taking off, the crackle of radios emitting message traffic back and forth between unseen military units, and the unmistaken sounds of gunfire fill the senses. Many visitors quickly look up attempting to see the arriving or departing *choppers* that are not there. Often, they wince, or duck as a *gun fires* nearby. Some of the war veterans briefly feel back in-country, surrounded by effective physical memorabilia and the sounds of long ago. Most all visitors are experiencing a small bit of the sights and sounds of the Vietnam War in a setting recreating a typical fire support base, usually found scattered somewhere in that war zone in the Republic of Vietnam.

Fire support bases ranged in size and scope from temporary havens for safety to launch pads for patrols or assault sweeps, often called "search and destroy" missions against the enemy. Many of these bases contained support facilities for shelter, protection, creature comforts, communication facilities, medical-treatment facilities, resupply stores, and artillery emplacements. Some were Spartan, while others, by comparison, exotic.

★★★

The year 1968 was the year of the TET Offensive by the North Vietnamese (PANV) and Viet Cong (VC). It changed the war. Forever! The word TET is a shortened version of the Vietnamese New Year or Tết Nguyên Đán, the first day of spring. In 1968, it was the first country-wide, massive North Vietnamese and Viet Cong attack on almost every military installation, village, and cities in the Republic of Vietnam. It was a year that changed our country and our attitude.

★★★

USS *Laffey* was called "the ship that wouldn't die." After supporting the Allied invasion at Normandy, in 1944, the Laffey relocated to the Pacific and participated in the invasion of Okinawa. She was a picket ship protecting the outer ring of the massive invasion fleet. It was during this engagement that the desperate Japanese turned to its most lethal weapon, the kamikaze (*divine wind*) suicide bombers. On 14 April 1945, Laffey fought against twenty-two Japanese suicide bombers gunning down thirteen of the attacking aircraft, but being struck by six of the suicide aircraft. In addition to the six suicide bombers that hit her, the ship was also hit by four bombs. Thirty-two crewmen died in the attack, but the ship would not sink, it would not die. It continued to fight.

Laffey was also a participant in the Korean War. She was decommissioned in 1975, after operating in the Mediterranean for several years. Many of the visitors to Patriots Point served on the USS *Laffey*, at different times and different places.

★★★

The number one attraction at the Maritime and Naval Museum at Patriots Point is the USS *Yorktown*. She was commissioned 15 April 1943, and decommissioned on 27 June 1970. In between, she served in numerous engagements during the War in the Pacific of World War II, during the Korean War, and off the coast of Vietnam during the Vietnam War. Daily, hundreds of visitors tour *Yorktown's* flight deck, hanger deck, and her massive, twisting passageways and compartments below decks. Many veterans, Navy and Marine, who served on her in war and peace, are drawn to their old billeting areas, battle stations, or assigned work spaces. Many of them relate their captivating stories from their times while they were serving on this "*giant, modern vessel* of her day." *Yorktown's* length is about 850 feet, with a beam of about 100 feet, and a crew, including aviation personnel, of about 3,000, while today's USS *Ronald Reagan*, CVN-76, is 1092 feet in length, with a beam of 252 feet, and a crew, including aviation personnel, of 5,680. But, in her day, *Yorktown* was a massive aircraft carrier. Indeed, she was a *Fighting Lady.*

She sports many interesting and historical artifacts and displays below decks and within the bays of the hanger deck and aboard her flight deck, aircraft representing many eras abound. Also on the hanger deck is the National Medal of Honor Museum. Below decks reveal unique modifications within an array of compartments and passageways laden with the best machinery, facilities, and equipment available from 1943 through 1972. Modifications reveal an interesting and informative display of various ship's artifacts, photographs, videos, and artwork telling the story of the history of naval warfare.

Young visitors, either as individuals or groups, such as boy scouts, sea cadets, explorer post, and others, often spend a night or two aboard this Navy aircraft carrier. They depart with a better understanding of how the men of the crew lived, and why they served their country.

★★★

Patriots Point's Maritime and Naval Museum's motto is "WALK IN THE STEPS OF HEROES!" That motto is more than a saying. It is a fact. As the visitor ascends or descends the many ladders aboard

USS *Yorktown* and USS *Laffey,* some will perhaps catch a mental image, an emotional glimpse for a brief or lingering time, of young men responding to the loud, resounding, squawking call of, "Pilot's, man your planes!" while flight garbed pilots rush from the ready room to the flight deck, to rise and meet the challenge of that day. Or, upon departing a compartment to the deck of the destroyer, one may sense a sound echoing throughout the ship, sounding off: "Battle stations! Battle stations! All hands, man your battle stations!" A brief image of gun turrets rotating toward an unseen enemy, sailors on watch scanning the skies through powerful binoculars, shouting and pointing toward dots in the sky, as guns began to belch flame and shells clatter on the steel deck, plants itself deep in your mind for a fleeting second, the effects perhaps lingering still. You are actually *walking* in the steps of heroes.

Walking through *The Vietnam Experience*, of reconstructed physical structures, and relocated machines of war from a time and place of long ago and far away, the sights combine with unmistakable sounds conjuring images of a typical combat support fire-base manned by another generation of young American patriots. You are walking in the footsteps of soldiers, sailors, Marines, and airmen, and yes, a few "Coasties" of the US Coast Guard, performing their duty during the War in Vietnam. Firebases or fire support bases were usually hastily constructed compounds away from major, larger, more permanent military cantonments, and offered support to infantry, or river patrol units operating from it to find, fix (in place), and destroy the enemy forces opposing them. From this compound, daily patrols frequently depart searching for the elusive enemy forces. These patrols usually returned to the same compound, depending on their mission, for safety and security. Artillery within these fire bases could support the sweeping infantry units as required. Also into this compound entered occasional land vehicles and numerous helicopters. Some of these mobile machines and aircraft would depart quickly, while others would sometime linger for an undetermined period of time. These arriving and departing machines of war would bring in supplies, mail and packages from home, wounded personnel, additional replacement personnel, or would evacuate the dead or wounded and/or other personnel and equipment as the situation dictated. For many servicemen these fire bases were their home away from home.

No two firebases were alike; however, they usually contained a command bunker for the command staff, often a captain, or depending on size, perhaps a lieutenant colonel, his communications necessities, sandbag bunkers and fighting positions for protection and defense from attacks, an aid station, and a helicopter landing space (pad) made up the fire base structures. Some were more sophisticated, containing a mess tent or structure, hut (hooch) or tent living quarters, fuel and ammunition storage, more exotic communications facilities, and the ever present sandbag bunkers for protective measures. Much depended on the mission of the base and the planned permanency of its longevity.

Though it is a recreated structure, walking through this *Experience* one may often feel dwelling here the spirits of men who lived and died during that war in Vietnam. For some—it has become hallowed ground.

As a note of interest, *Yorktown* and Vietnam firebases in general, have something unusual in common. Ann Margaret, the celebrated actress and entertainer, visited and performed on and at both of 'em during her 1966 tour in Vietnam. And, years later she revisited the *Yorktown* at Patriots Point during a movie shoot in South Carolina. During that visit, she met a former sailor who was on *Yorktown* in 1966, when she entertained the crew with song and dance.

As one may imagine, there is a mighty cast of people and organizations behind this massive and vital operation of the Maritime and Naval Museum at Patriots Point. At the top are the Board of Directors made up of nine members. The Executive Director and Assistant Executive Director control the functioning of numerous managers, coordinators, and directors of various departments that manage and control the daily functioning of The Maritime and Naval Museum at Patriots Point.

Neatly folded into this massive organization is the unique crop of volunteers. These stories are from and about those volunteers:

CHAPTER 1

DICK WHITAKER PATRIOTS POINT VOLUNTEER

★★★

AS TOLD IN HIS OWN WORDS, AND RETREIVED FROM DOCUMENTS PROVIDED TO THE EDITOR OF THIS ANTHOLOGY

DICK WHITAKER PHOTO PROPERTY OF EDITOR

Dick Whitaker was born three years before the Great Depression fell across the entire United States and most of the rest of the world, and was six-years-old when Franklin Roosevelt was elected President of the United States for the first time. He grew into maturity as roughly

300,000 young unmarried men entered the Civilian Conservation Corps (CCC's) to escape unemployment and abject poverty sweeping across America, and as World War II burst upon the world stage, ending the economic depression. By the time he was nearing graduation from high school, he, like thousands of other young American males, knew what loomed shortly after their eighteenth birthday—the "greetings" letter from the draft board. It was war-time, and young, able bodied males had a legal, and for many, a moral obligation to their country. Realizing the obvious, he decided not to wait.

Most young Americans of his time were eager to do their part in the war effort. Almost all America was, in some way, contributing to winning the war. For the first time, women worked in our bustling factories alongside the men. They also ferried aircraft from factory to war zones, and volunteered for military service; while it was the young men who would face our foes on the field of battle. At seventeen-years-old, Dick wanted to join his friends who had enlisted in large numbers. He wanted to do his part. **"Whitaker himself yearned to join Saugerties's recruits already certified as heroes."**[1] On almost a whim, without discussing it with his parents, he departed his home town of Saugerties, NY. Well. Wait! Let him tell the story:

"I had decided that I wanted to go into the military and I wanted it to be the Marines. I knew from experience that once you received that draft notice, you were going into the Army. I didn't want that, so, one day in December 1943, without anyone knowing, I took a bus up to the Induction Station in Albany. There, I went into the Marine Corps recruiting office and signed up for the Marines. I signed all the paperwork, and passed the physical; however, because I was seventeen, the recruiting sergeant gave me a form and told me to take it home and have my parents sign it. I went home with the paper, walked into the house,

1 Tennozan: *The Battle of Okinawa and the Atomic Bomb.* George Feifer, 1992, Ticknor & Fields, p. 35

and presented the paper to my parents while telling them what I had done.

"They were not at all happy with my actions. My father was blunt. He said to me, 'You're not going into the Marine Corps!' And, that was that. He simply had forbidden it. Period! I remember that even our minister and my school principal endorsed my father's decision. The bottom line is I didn't get any signatures on that paper.

"Right after my graduation from high school in June 1944 (I had turned eighteen on 13 March 1944), I received in the mail the draft notice to report to the same Induction Station I had been to earlier. This time as an inductee into the US Army. I was not a happy camper. I arrived at the Induction Station in Albany, and got in line with all the other draftees being processed into the US Army. As I got closer to the front of the line, I saw that same Marine recruiter who had sent me home with the papers for my parents to sign. He was walking out of his office and saw me."

"What happened to you?" he casually remarked to me.

"They wouldn't sign." I responded.

"Do you still want the Corps?" he asked.

"Got drafted." I held up my draft notice for him to see.

"If you still want the Marine Corps, come with me."

"Yeah. But, I've been drafted."

"Don't worry about it. I'll fix it."

"As I followed, we went back to his office. There was another person there whose parents would not sign his approval for enlistment. I signed some papers, and then the two of us were given chits for meals and a night's stay at the YMCA. At 0815 the next day, I was sworn into the Marine Corps. I was now a Marine on my way, on a course that would take me to Parris Island, Camp Lejeune, San Diego, Guadalcanal, Okinawa, Guam, and China. But first, I was a recruit at the Marine Corps boot camp at Parris Island."

So, that's how a young Dick Whitaker became a Marine. To look at his home office, one would assume that Dick Whitaker lived his entire adult life in the Corps of Marines. Marine Corps books, photos and mementoes adorn the office walls and tops of his desk and other tables in his office in his home in Mt Pleasant, SC. And the reality, Dick was on active duty for only a couple of years, but they were filled with constant training, combat on Okinawa, and, finally, a pretty nice billet in China.

John Lejeune coined the phrase *Once a Marine, always a Marine.* Dick has been a Marine since that day he raised his right hand. The Marine Corps established the foundation for all else he accomplished in his life. And that foundation was honed like fire hones steel in some of the most savage combat during the War in the Pacific, before he returned to his New York State hometown of Saugerties. As the great radio announcer, Paul Harvey repeated time and time again: *And, now, the rest of the story*:

I asked, **"How about it, Dick? Why the Marines?"**

His response was, "Look, I was seventeen-years-old at that time. Impressionable? Yes! Very impressionable. It was probably those John Wayne movies more than anything," he relinquished candidly.

He had a week's leave after boot camp, and two month's infantry training at Camp Lejeune before being shipped to the West Coast in December 1944.

"I spent my nineteenth birthday on Guadalcanal," he reminisced. "We were part of the 29th Replacement Draft."

Dick Whitaker landed on Okinawa with the third wave on Red Beach 2, unopposed by the Japanese, on Easter Sunday, Aprils Fool's Day, the first of April 1945. It was also Easter Sunday. The men of the landing force penetrated ahead of schedule so fast that by the time Dick arrived with the third wave, the problem became one of getting the massive supplies and equipment off the beach and up to the advancing troops. Dick's replacement draft was pressed into service as part of a 5,000 man working party to get the supplies and equipment to where it could be used. These beach parties were broken up bit by bit as replacements were needed. Eventually Dick found himself, along with a few others, assigned to Fox Company, 2nd Battalion, 29th Marines, a regiment of the 6th Marine Division.

The United States Marines had evolved and developed from a cadre pre-war force in 1940 of some 55,000 Marines mushrooming to a force of nearly half a million men by the time the last battle of World War II was fought on Okinawa. The Marine Corps ended the war with six divisions and five aircraft wings. It was, at that time, the most powerful amphibious force the world has ever known.

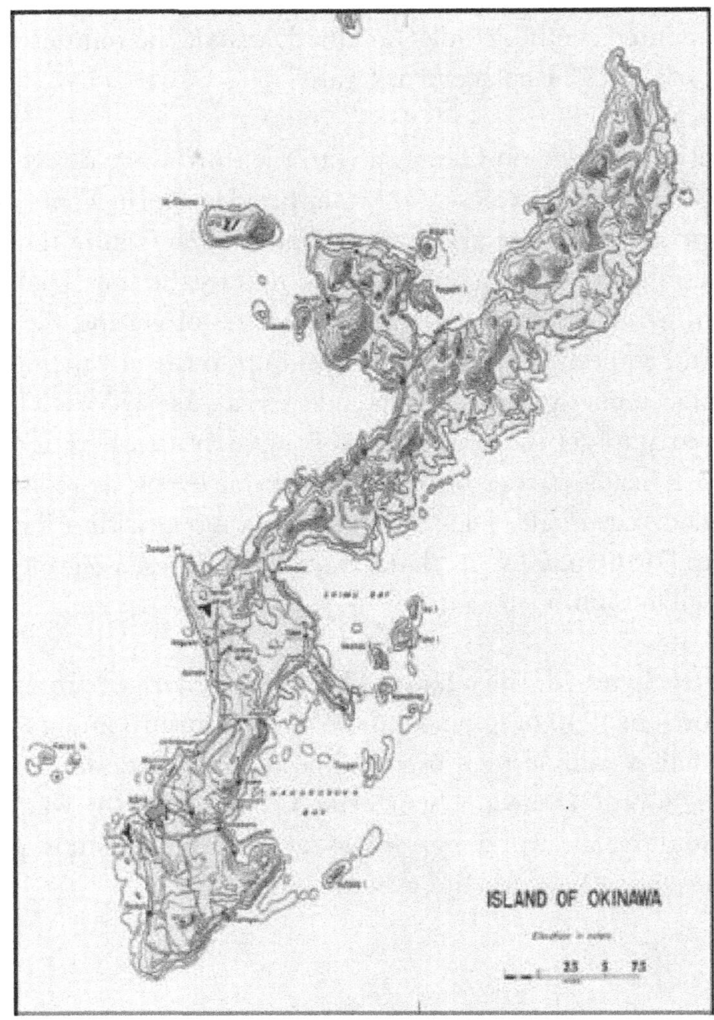

Map of Okinawa from Internet

Okinawa was tactically important because it gave the allies a launch pad close to Japan for the planned and pending invasion of Japan proper. At that time, it seemed the only way to end the war was to invade and conquer all of Japan. Okinawa was vital to those plans for the conquest of Japan. Okinawa is sixty-five miles long and only two miles at its most narrow location and forty miles across its widest width. The invasion forces were to land in the middle of the island and then turn north and south.

Red Beach, where Dick came ashore, was in the Yonton [Yomitan] area. He described to me that some distance from where they landed was a coral-made runway. He and his buddy tried to dig a foxhole after darkness, but were unable to do so because of the coral. At daybreak, they discovered they were on that runway, and moving only four or five feet would have put them on soil where they could have dug that foxhole.

> ***Yours truly, the Executive Editor of this publication, was very familiar of where Dick and his buddy were located because I had several tours on Okinawa, lasting cumulatively for six and a half years, and often drove my car on that old coral runway many times. As far as I know, it is still there.***

The invasion force came ashore with little resistance. That resistance would come later. The 29th Marines moved north toward the Motubu peninsula. Fighting was relatively light until the Japanese resistance was overcome. Then, rather than a respite from constant combat, the 29th Marines were ordered to move south to join the US Army forces attempting to take the Suri Ridge areas overlooking Naha. Dick's Fox Company went into the attack in the Sugar Loaf area, attacking strong Japanese positions for days until his Fox Company was reduced by casualties from a force of 264 men, down to only sixty-one effectives remaining. On 17 May 1945, after coming off the ridgeline again and being ordered to dig in . . . Well, again . . . let Dick tell his story:

"By now it was dusk and John [Senterfitt] and I knew we had to stay where we were for the night. We found a shallow foxhole on the north slope of Queen Hill and using our entrenching tools we proceeded to make it deeper. When we finished digging, John lay down in the bottom of the hole and lit a cigarette. I stuck my entrenching tool [into the ground] near the edge of the hole, put my feet in the hole and leaned back against the entrenching tool handle, as if it were the back of a chair, to also light a cigarette. When I found my matches were wet, I leaned down to get a light from John. As I bent forward, I steadied myself by grasping the handle of my shovel [entrenching tool], at that same instant, a bullet hit the shovel's handle and also my left hand."

Dick thought his wound was minor and spent the night in his position. After a corpsman checked on him at daybreak, he was evacuated to an aide station for treatment. Two days later he rejoined his company. Upon rejoining his unit, the company commander's runner asked Dick to take the radio and to become his runner as the previous runner had been killed. Dick became the C.O.'s runner. Thus began a long relationship that would last a lifetime. Dick took a bit of time to explain his relationship with his company commander, Robert Sherer:

"I was with lieutenant (later captain) Sherer constantly. He was a great officer. Never wore rank insignia, never carried a map case, didn't carry a carbine like many officers, and never carried binoculars. To do so made you a prime target for Japanese snipers. Like us low ranked enlisted, he carried an M-1 rifle. Then, on one particular day, we were descending a slope when the captain, for some unknown reason, stopped, reached into his utility shirt and removed a map. Right in front of my eyes he unfolded it and began to read it. He just stood there reading that map with his rifle slung upside down by the sling over his shoulder.

"I was carrying a Thompson sub machine gun; I'll tell you later how I got that particular weapon. Well," he continued. "I looked toward a sugar cane field on a ridgeline to our left front, and suddenly out from those sugar canes burst this Japanese soldier. He was naked except for boots, G-string-diaper-like briefs, and a steel helmet. He was running toward the captain. I could see a hand grenade in each of his hands."

"A suicide charge," I stated.

"Yep. It was that. Apparently, he had not received the word that his commanding general had committed *hara-kiri, or Seppuku* (cutting the belly open resulting in death), and that the Japanese on Okinawa had surrendered"

"And, what happened?"

"I brought my Thompson up and fired a burst hitting him several times. He flew sideways into a ditch as both grenades exploded."

"You saved your captain's life."

"I don't think of it that way. I was doing what I was trained to do," he stated emphatically. When George Feifer was writing *Tennozan: The Battle of Okinawa and the Atomic Bomb*, I asked him to not write about that particular event."

"Dick, when you are the person whose life is the one saved, you never forget the person who saved it, and I'd like to write about it," I stated.

"Alright," he responded.

"So, tell me more about your captain."

There's a lot to tell, but one thing in particular you should be aware of. That Marine officer was the only one of eight original officers in my company (F/2/29) who was not killed or wounded requiring evacuation. Even four or five replacement officers were killed or seriously wounded requiring evacuation. One officer joined us in the morning and was killed that night. Well, to continue, when the fighting was over on Okinawa, we went to Guam to train for the invasion of the Japanese homeland. Then, the two atomic bombs. They saved my life and thousands of others on both sides. As luck would have it, the 6th Marine Division was ordered to China. One day, the captain walks up to me and says, 'Whitaker, I'm going home. I got the points. But, don't worry. I've taken care of you. You'll be in good hands.' I thought that was the last time I would ever see my captain."

"What happened?"

"I was an orderly; some may call it a *gofer,* to a colonel as we were now deployed to China to accept the surrender of thousands of Japanese soldiers. I lived in a hotel. Can you believe that? We were in Tsingtao, China for a long time. Most of the time I had a day on and a day off. I left in May 1946, and arrived home on Memorial Day. But, I'm getting ahead of myself. As the colonel's orderly, I had the *life of Riley.* On one particular occasion, we went in a landing craft up the coast of China in the North China Sea on a four or five month training mission. Once, we were met by a Chinese Army general who invited us, the colonel, a *Life Magazine* reporter, our DUKW (an amphibious vehicle) driver, and me, to a dinner at the mayor's house in Ping Lai. It was an elaborate affair. The dinner had all kinds of plates, glasses, and silverware on the table. I just watched the colonel and used the fork or glass he was using. My buddy on my left was drinking from a finger bowl. We were grungy and smelled to high-heaven.

"You deserved that assignment after Okinawa."

"Perhaps."

"How did you meet your captain again?"

"Weirdest thing. I was back in the States, at a subway station in Long Island. I'm sitting in my car, when from my rear this guy walked past me. Don't ask me why. Can't explain it. As I looked at his backside, his walk, his shoulders, I recognized him. I had walked behind that captain on Okinawa. I know his walk. I got out to follow him. It took me a while to catch up to him. I called out 'hey, *Scissors*!' That was his radio code name on Okinawa. Bob Sherer turned around. We have been close friends all this time. He died not long ago. He had placed a telephone call to me, and we talked briefly. It was the day he died."

It was clear to me that Dick had lost his best friend. There was a brief silence, so I changed the subject. **"How'd you get that Thompson on Okinawa?"** I asked.

"Well we had come across this observation post. Our guys. They were in communication with navy ships at sea and were looking for targets or taking incoming radio calls from units with a request for naval gun-fire to be fired on some targets. One of the guys called out to us, 'Hey, come look at this.' I go over, took the field-glasses, and looked over to the next ridgeline. There, as clear as day, are two Japanese setting up a table. It looked like a ping-pong table, but was perhaps a map table. There they were, in plain sight. So, this Marine starts calling for naval gun fire. I thought, almost aloud—*you gonna have a battleship kill two Japanese*? Yep. That's what they're going to do. So, somewhere out there on that big crowded ocean a battlewagon fires a salvo on this target. Just happened, there was a short-round in that salvo. It goes off near us and blows me over the side of a hill and I slid down to the bottom ending up on a road somewhere down below, right near a passing medical jeep. A doctor asked if I was hurt. Now I can't hear a thing, and my rifle stock is broken at the grip. Otherwise I think I'm alright, but they sent me out to a hospital ship to be examined. I was released the next day and returned to my unit. I'm alright, but I needed another rifle, but, when I got back to my unit, all they came up with was a Reising sub-machine gun. Totally unreliable weapon."

"Amazing! What luck you're having." We both laughed.

"Well, me and another Marine were moving back from the beach to somewhere else when we came across an Army field kitchen. There's this Army sergeant inside opening big tin cans of ham. Now, we Marines were almost starving. I lost 20 pounds on Okinawa. We walk inside the Mess-Tent, and ask the sergeant if we could have one of the cans of ham to take back to our unit. Whereupon, this guy starts giving us a hard-time. Right in the middle of his tirade my buddy turned on the Army sergeant. Here we are a couple of tired, dirty, hungry Marines and this guy is all alone in this Mess Tent. Nobody else around. We must have looked pretty desperate to this sergeant, not knowing what we may do. My Marine buddy picked up one of the cans of ham and we began to back out of the tent western saloon style. That's when I saw this Tommy gun hanging from the center tent pole. I needed a good gun, so I took it. That's how I got the Tommy gun."

"What about after the war, after you returned from China to the States?"

"I just hung out for a couple of years. Then I enrolled in college at Syracuse University. Earned a BS in Journalism and Public Relations. Joined the Shell Oil Company after graduation. But, later Syracuse University offered me a position of Director of Development and Public Relations at Utica College of Syracuse University. Then in 1962, I became Director of Development at Kent School, a private boarding school in Kent, Connecticut. I remained there for twenty-seven years."

"And after that?"

"My wife and I sailed. From a condo where we lived in at Oriental, North Carolina, we sailed down the east coast on a thirty-two foot Bayfield Cutter, and on over to the Bahamas a few times. It was great, but it had to come to an end. In 1998, we *Swallowed the Anchor* [sold the boat] and moved to Mt Pleasant. I enjoy volunteering at Patriots Point. I enjoy helping visitors, and enjoy working with the other volunteers."

The Ashley River Creative Arts School fifth-grade class of students visiting Patriots Point gave Dick his most memorable experience while a volunteer. Several days after Dick escorted and briefed the students about World War II and his experiences in that war, he received letters of thanks from all sixty-seven visiting students enclosed in one large envelop. Dick read every one and responded in a letter to them all. Since that day in 2007, he has retained every one of those letters in a bound notebook. This event was featured in the summer of 2007 issue no. 5 of *Scuttlebutt* titled "The Whitaker Letters."

"You obviously have a deep affinity for the Corps."

"The Corps gave me direction. It is perhaps the foundation of my life."

As this writer departed the home of Dick Whitaker, we exchanged age old greeting and salutation between Marines. The words are Semper Fi.

It was an honor to visit and interview Dick Whitaker. His generation is the product of the Great Depression, World War II, and the economic giant that followed called the American Dream that began at the end of that war. The news commentator, Tom Brokaw, has called this generation of Americans, *The Greatest Generation.* In his book, he describes why he coined the phrase that became his book title: *"In the spring of 1984, I went to the northwest of France, to Normandy, to prepare an NBC documentary on the fortieth anniversary of D-Day, the massive and daring Allied invasion of Europe that marked the beginning of the end of Adolf Hitler's Third Reich. There, I underwent a life-changing experience. As I walked the beaches with the American veterans who had returned for this anniversary, men in their sixties and seventies, and listened to their stories, I was deeply moved and profoundly grateful for all they had done. Ten years later, I returned to Normandy for the fiftieth anniversary of the invasion, and by then I had come to understand what this generation of Americans meant to history. It is, I believe, the greatest generation any society has ever produced."*

Indeed the America of the 1940s and 1950s was nourished by the feats of those mostly young men who rose from the economic despair of the Great Depression, marched to the sound of the gun to defeat the forces of the Axis powers determined to enslave the world, then returned to their homeland, raise families, and created an economic, cultural, and spiritual giant. Such is the legacy of men like Dick Whitaker, a Marine Corps combat veteran, and a Patriots Point volunteer.

This story was constructed from face-to-face conversations with Dick Whitaker from documents he provided to me, and, most importantly, after reading the publication by author George Feifer titled *Tennozan*. While I did not have the fortune of being Dick Whitaker's long time neighbor and fellow wood-splitter, like George Feifer, as a Marine combat veteran of the Vietnam War, and a career (twenty-six years) Marine, I not only understand Dick's discussions with me, I can also feel them. This is a small, but valuable, writing project about the volunteers at the Patriots Point Naval and Maritime Museum, the subject is priceless.

On another more personal note, on page 495 of the book *Tennozan,* the author mentions in a footnote, Sergeant J.R. Aichie delivering four Okinawan babies during the Okinawa campaign. There was a Colonel Jim R. Achlie, my Chief of Staff at Marine Corps Base, Camp Butler, Okinawa, who, as a sergeant, had delivered four babies on Okinawa during the 1945 fighting. One of those babies grew up to either own or manage the Bank of the Ryukyu's. He and our colonel were great friends.

Re: email Fwd: Marine Corps Combat Veteran Dick Whitaker

RALPH BATES <ralynbat@bellsouth.net>
To:Addresses
Bcc:ralynbat@bellsouth.net
Apr 17 at 10:41 AM

Am sitting in the parking lot of Roper St Frances, Roper Hospice Cottage. Just concluded a visit to Dick Whitaker in room 13. This Marine was in bed, unresponsive, appearing to be in a deep sleep. I made no attempt to awaken him. Briefly, these are my thoughts before heading back to my home:

This Marine radioman for the CO of Fox Company, 29th Marines, in continuous combat for eighty-eight days, wounded, and instrumental in saving his commanding officers life in the closing days of the final battle of World War II, Okinawa, now appears gaunt and frail. But within that old body burns the flame of the epitome of "The Greatest Generation." It's called service.

He served his Country and his Corps of Marines, returned to civilian persuasions, and lived a fruitful life, raising a family and prospering in the freedoms he fought for, and unselfishly gave to his fellow countrymen in his and the generations to follow.

Last we talked, last week, he sported a USMC sweatshirt and wearing a Marine Corps cover (hat for the uninformed), he reminisced, with Paul Watters and me, about those days so long ago that set the foundation for his good life and good fortune.

In his service to his Corps and Country he established a lasting legacy. As a volunteer at Patriots Point and a member of Lowcountry Leathernecks, he fostered and passed that legacy to countless generations of others, especially the young, our future pool from which leaders are drawn. He accomplished his mission.

Semper Fi, Dick.
Stoney

Sent from my iPhone

A few scant hours after this email was sent, to quote Mac Burdette, "Dick is with his Marines in heaven."

The old Marine took his last breath on earth. A few days later, his wife, joined him.

CHAPTER 2

VOLUNTEER MARK NADOBNY

★★★

MARK NADOBNY: PHOTO PROPERTY OF AUTHOR

Mark Nadobny volunteers at times on the same day(s) I volunteer at the Naval and Maritime Museum at Patriots Point. Our first musings regarding his part of my anthology *Short Rations From Patriots Point Volunteers* was at Dunleavy's Pub on Sullivan's Island. After a *few*, I knew there was no way he would not be included in this book. Mark is one of a kind. He reminds me of the phrase, "When life gives you lemons, make lemonade." I'll explain later.

Ralph Stoney Bates, Sr., author/editor.

At the "Point," some of the old salts still refer to him as "skivvy-waver," a term applied to the signalmen of the US Navy. That was the guy seen in old Navy films who stood on the ship and signaled others by displaying hand-held signal flags, or flashing a special shutter-light called the Aldis-Lamp, signaling ship-to-ship, or ship-to-shore. The Navy disestablished the rating in 2003. The end of another era. Mark was the last of a kind.

Mark entered the US Navy after completing Seaford High School on Long Island, plus earning an Associated Degree from Nassau Community College in Garden City, New York, and completing a Bachelor's Degree in Education from State University of New York. Possessing a B.A. in Education, or any other discipline, Mark could have entered the Navy under several programs as a Navy Officer Candidate; instead, he entered as an enlisted sailor for two-years active duty and six-years as a reserve. His service was from 1991 through 1999.

Mark's story is, in a way, a feast or famine missive. He was sent to sunny Orlando, Florida instead of snowy Great Lakes, Illinois for his boot camp. He began his navy life in the Deck Division as a simple deck-hand, chipping paint, manning brooms and swabs, and performing other minimal, but necessary tasks. He rose from that occasion to become something above those simple tasks. He became a Signalman. He also had a most interesting short stint as a public relations operative on the waters of the Great Lakes, addressing groups or individuals visiting his ship. When the ship relocated to the Caribbean to become involved in "*chasing drug runners*," and, also in the Caribbean, participating in Haitian intervention, including imposing a naval blockade of Haiti's major port, while, at the same time, and providing humanitarian assistance to the suffering people of that nation. Then, relocating to the home port of the Charleston Navy Base, his Navy days were anything but dull and routine.

His first love, other than his wife Kathleen, was education, while at the same time his love for his country compelled his enlistment in the Navy. This may sound corny to some; but Mark is one of those old-fashioned

American patriots. He could have continued, after his earned degrees, to excel in additional pursuits for self-improvement, and probably rolled right into becoming a noted educator; but, he chose to serve his country before self.

After serving his two-year active duty gaining the rank of 3rd Class Petty Officer, he utilized his earned GI Bill to continue his education, earning a second B.A. in Social Science from the University of Cincinnati and a M.A. in Secondary Education from Northern Kentucky University. Not yet finished, he began a graduate program in Theology at Xavier University of Cincinnati, but instead relocated to Charleston in 2006. He continued graduate courses in Education at the College of Charleston.

As one may surmise, Mark lives and breathes education. His start in this life's endeavor was just a bit unusual. He began his first stint as a teacher by teaching in a maximum security prison, not as a resident, but as a high-school-GED teacher of inmates. Thus, Mark entered the teaching profession behind the walls of a maximum security prison, attempting to offer even a slight chance that his efforts would provide one or more of these inmates a better life than crime had offered them. Mark called it, "starting at the bottom." Yet, it was a noble start. After eighteen months he did get a position as a high school teacher in Cincinnati. This time, it was outside the prison walls.

Mark met his wife, Kathleen, at the Naval Base of Charleston in 1993. It was a love at first sight meeting. They met in March. They dated for ten days. He departed aboard ship, returning in May. She was on the pier when the ship returned. He proposed on 8 August. They married nine days later on 16 August. They make movies about this kind of setting. They have two children. Their first, Samuel Elliot bears the name of Mark's ship *USS Samuel Elliot Morrison* (FFG-13). Now, there's a guy who loved his navy. That was his first ship in the Navy. Their second child, a daughter, is Hannah Elizabeth.

Mark has had, and is still having, a varied and successful career in education. It's in his blood, just as the US Navy is also in his blood. As an educator, he has won many awards and accolades. He has traveled extensively. This part-time bartender (remember, our first meeting was at Dunleavy's Pub on Sullivan's Island, not far from where he proposed to Kathleen) has come a long way from deck-hand, prison school teacher, and Long Island high school graduate. A long, long way!

He has a deep affinity for Navy ships. He still speaks and sometime writes of the "scent of paint and oil," and of, "the feel of déjà vu when walking lower [Yorktown] passageways . . . " Yes, NAVY is still within him. Of his volunteer duties, he writes, "All of this," he reminisces, "in one way or another brings me back to my Navy days, a decision in my life for which I hold no regrets and one I would repeat with without reservation."

Mark Nadobny is the epitome of the Volunteers at the Naval and Maritime Museum at Patriots Point.

After I gave Mark a copy of my first edit, based on our conversation at the *Irish Watering Hole* on Sullivan's Island, he had more he wanted to add. At this point, let us let him tell it in his own words:

"I think you really nailed it, but I would like to add that every elder male in my family has served in the military—grandfathers, uncles, cousins and my dad, a Navy Corpsman who served in Vietnam. In fact, every branch of the military has been served with members of my family. Yes, I wanted to serve my country, this was and still is important, but I also wanted to continue a family tradition. A strong family tradition. It continues even today as my youngest brother, Tommy, is currently serving active duty in the Air Force.

"While on my ship and waiting on the chow-line I remember a fellow shipmate (who had learned of my background in education with all the degrees, he asked me why I enlisted in the Navy? My answer was simple and to the point—**I wanted to serve my country!** Yes, this does seem old fashioned (as you implied) but that›s who I am. Even twenty-five years later, that same shipmate of mine still reminds me of how impressed he was by my answer.

"Yes, the Navy was good to me and it still is. I absolutely love being a veteran and am so grateful that I made that apparent unorthodox decision so many years ago.

"I attended my thirtieth high school reunion a few years ago and learned that out of my class of 275, I am the only military veteran. My hometown of Seaford, NY is patriotic, however few, very few ever do join the military. Perhaps, it is simply a sign of the times. Upon learning this—a sense of pride overcame me. I can't explain it. It just did.

"Oh, by-the-way, I met my wife at the Wild Wing Cafe on the Market (in Charleston, SC) on St. Patrick's Day of 1993 and yes, we were married by August 16th of 1993 (with a two-month deployment in between, and that deployment happened only ten days after our meeting). Our courtship was conducted via the "old fashion way," by letter writing and awaiting the old fashioned "Mail Call" while on that two-month Legal-Ops deployment in the Caribbean.

"Thanks for all your efforts on this anthology! Looking forward to the publishing of this book."

CHAPTER 3

PAUL WATTERS: PATRIOTS POINT VOLUNTEER

PAUL WATTERS: PHOTO PROPERTY OF AUTHOR

I have been asked by Ralph Stoney Bates, another volunteer here at Patriots Point Maritime and Naval Museum, to tell a bit about myself. It is for a book he is writing about many of the volunteers here. Alright! Here goes!

I first saw the light of day on 1 June 1944, in Cleveland, Ohio. When I was four-years-old, my family moved to Hartford, Connecticut. Yes, they took their four-year-old son and six-year-old daughter with them. My parents were the adventurous type, so when my father was between jobs, aka, unemployed, they decided to "go out west" to find greener pastures. So, in 1950, my sister and I were packed in the back seat of a 1948 Oldsmobile "woody" station wagon with all our worldly possessions and we made a two-week trip across the country following the classic Route 66 west. We finally saw the Pacific Ocean and sunny beaches of Southern California and my parents decided it was a good place to stake a new claim. We found a home in Downey, California, a suburb of Los Angeles, where my father, a mechanical engineer, quickly found work in the aviation defense industry. I graduated in 1961 from Earl Warren High School now called simply Warren High School, so named after the former Chief Justice of the Supreme Court —a native son of Downey, California. Then I attended Whittier College, Whittier California, graduating in 1965, with a degree in Political Science.

Receiving my anticipated draft notice immediately upon graduation from college and having orders to Fort Ord in California for Army basic training, I decided to enlist in the Navy instead. I have never regretted it. I qualified for flight training and made my way to Pensacola, Florida for flight school, of course after passing the rigorous pre-flight training, some under the tutorage of Marine Corps Drill Instructors (read: *Pressure Cooker, Forging Naval Officers Through Marine*

Leadership, by John Crouch, 1st Sergeant, USMC), eventually receiving my wings of gold and assigned to fly helicopters. My entire graduating class of '75 got orders to HA (L)-3, (Helicopter Attack (Light) Squadron Three, the famous Seawolves, in Viet Nam. After several months of advanced training, I arrived in Viet Nam and spent the next year flying helicopter gunships providing airborne protection for the river boats operating in the rivers and canals of the Mekong Delta.

Yours truly, as a lieutenant (jg), was assigned to Detachment 6, a two helo gunship, sixteen-man detachment (eight pilots, eight maintenance/ gunners), forward deployed to an Advanced Tactical Support Base (ATSB), located at the mouth of a wide river flowing into the Gulf of Thailand. The base was comprised of floating barges that supplied maintenance and support for the river boats, and was our command post. The Seawolves were there to provide aerial cover and gun ship protection. We had a rudimentary base camp, in a fenced compound located across the river from the barges. We had two eight-man hootch's (South East Asia huts) built on stilts over a marsh, and a nearby landing pad our helicopters took-off and landed upon. Our compound was in close proximity to the village of Song Ong Doc, and, over time, we became friendly with the villagers who were mostly families of rice farmers and fishermen. Small kids were always hanging around our hootch (hooch) and we eventually became friends with them.

On one particular day, I was sitting on the back porch of our hooch, which is a tin roofed, and primitive plywood hut used by US troops during the Vietnam War, and a few of the kids were hanging around so I started talking to them. Although we didn't share a common language, we had fun making gestures and pointing to things (parts of the body were popular) giving them words in English and they would tell me what it was in Vietnamese. One thing led to another and I decided to try to teach them how to play the "rock, paper, scissor" game. After a few minutes of gestures and giggling trying to get them to understand the game, one of the kids suddenly figured it out and excitedly explained to the others and the game was on!

Needless to say that became the best thing that ever happened to them (and to us), and we had almost daily contests with the whole crew, until the fateful night of 16 October 1970:

I was sound asleep in my mosquito-net-covered bunk in that plywood hut; with seven other guys in the hootch we shared, when the night was shattered by a huge explosion and massive cloud of dust. We had just been hit by either a mortar or rocket, followed by rapid rifle fire and more explosions. We were under ground attack by the bad guys! We all scrambled out of bed and ran for the sand-bagged bunker located just behind our hootch. We had an M-60 aimed out the bunker window at the perimeter of our compound and my job was to load the ammo from a box on the floor. I grabbed the ammo belt and tried to get it in the feed tray, but my hands were shaking so bad I kept dropping it. All hell was breaking loose outside. Then, the fuel tanks on the floating barges just across the river from us exploded, after taking direct hits from mortars and rocket fire. The PBR's (Patrol Boat River) and Swift Boats had gotten underway and were retuning fire along the opposite river bank. My flight leader yelled that we had to try to get the birds in the air so we ran back thru the hootch and ran about thirty yards down a raised wooden walkway from the hootch to the landing pad where our birds were waiting—all the time taking heavy fire from across the river. I jumped in the first helo on a dead run and hit the battery switch to start the engine. Suddenly, I realized that my crew chief – always diligent in having the bird ready for a quick night launch – had all the exterior light switches set in the "on" position so when I hit the battery I lit up like a Christmas tree, immediately drawing additional green tracer fire! I franticly starting turning off the lights, while, at the same time starting the engine, when my door gunner jumped into the back of the bird, bringing the deadly .50 cal. machine gun into action, raking the perimeter where the fire was coming from–almost at point blank range by this time. The other crew had reached their bird and we turned up and launched, with every gun blazing away as soon as we were in a hover. We started to attack the bad guys with suppressive fire all along the river bank and kept at it until we ran out of ammo and got low on fuel. Due to the loss of our fuel during the attack, we then headed up the river to an Army field at Ca Mau to rearm and refuel. Thus began several long hours of hot action that didn't stop until daylight. The guys who had to stay on the ground when we launched, were picked up by a PBR and taken up river to a secure location where we met up with them later. We were very fortunate not to have lost any of our guys and had no serious injuries, but we did have a lot of new bullet holes in our helos. As a result of the severe damage our compound had received from the attack, we were forced to abandon it, and moved the whole detachment off-shore taking up residence aboard the USS *Garrett County*, a WWII era LST. That vessel became our new home for the next six months. That experience alone, with more details is worth another long story! And I do have stories:

THE ARMY COLONEL STORY

When I was within a few weeks of the end of my tour, I was brought in from the detachment to fly "milk runs" at the home squadron until my departure date. In other words, nobody was supposed to be shooting at me anymore. It was just a few days before my departure and I had one more flight to do on the schedule. I was to fly to a remote outpost and pick up a senior Vietnamese Army officer and take him to another location. It was a long flight over bad-guy country and I wasn't very happy about it, but off I went. We arrived at the pick-up and three people were waiting for a ride—the Vietnamese officer and his staff guy and another guy wanting a ride someplace else. He had a flight helmet and army fatigues on and a very Asian face and build, so I thought it was another VN officer looking for a free ride with the US Navy. But I said ok, let's go, and we took off. During the long flight back, my co-pilot and I were discussing, over the ICS intercom, the fact that we were pissed at having to fly these xxxxing guys (gooks) around in a free taxi and how ready we were for the big Jet Plane outa' there. After dropping off the Vietnamese Army officer, I proceeded to the next stop for my unannounced passenger, which was a long hot flight in shitty weather, during which my copilot and I continued to voice our displeasure with what we were being asked to do for these freeloaders. We finally arrived at the destination and I landed on the helo pad and my passenger got out and walked up to my door of the helo. He had the dark visor of the flight helmet down over his eyes and a flack jacket on. He reached up and raised the visor, looked me in the eye and said as he reached up to shake my hand, "Thank you for ride, LT" - I glanced down at his uniform and saw birds on each collar and "[name omitted to placate publisher.] Colonel, US Army" on the flak jacket - he had been plugged into the intercom the whole flight and heard every word we said. He was a Korean-American Army officer - who knew?! The end of my career suddenly flashed in front of me - that was a real "Ah, sh*t" moment! The Freedom Bird couldn't get there any quicker!

Paul. When did you go on R&R?

Mid-way thru my deployment, I went to Hong Kong.

Why to Hong Kong?

I chose Hong Kong for my R&R because I had always dreamed about getting a monster stereo set (four huge speakers, reel-to-reel tape deck, powerful amp and turntable), and the China Fleet Club in HK was widely known to be the place to go! I caught a Northwest Orient Airlines flight out of Saigon for the seven hour flight. Shortly after takeoff, I was handed a menu to select my dinner choice and the food was prepared on a cart in front of me by a white uniformed steward and served with a chilled bottle of wine - talk about a great way to fly! I spent my first day in HK at the China Fleet Club - a big multistory warehouse type building with floor after floor of stereo gear of every kind known to man. I made my purchases and put them in the mail to San Diego. I also had three sets of dress uniforms and two sports jackets made at one of the many tailor shops that were on every street corner. I had my dress blue uniform jacket lined with red silk - very cool!

Returning back to Saigon from R and R in Hong Kong, I flew into Tan Son Nhut Airbase. I was hanging out in the air terminal wondering how I was going to get a ride back to my home squadron in Binh Thuy (about 130 miles to the south), when I saw a guy walk by me in a flight suit. He looked really familiar. I looked again and realized he was a classmate from flight school. I ran over and stopped him to say hi. After the normal hellos and greetings, he told me he was on his way to fly a C-47 (DC-3) down to a base not far from Binh Thuy and I could get a ride if I wanted. I accepted, grabbed my gear and hauled out to the already turning aircraft. I jumped in and strapped into a jump seat behind the pilot and co-pilot. As we taxied out I looked around the airplane and noticed stacks of cases of church song-hymnals and bibles strapped to the deck. That was the safest flight I ever had in-country!

Paul Watters: Photos above property of author

Arriving back to my unit, I was assigned as the senior Flight Team Leader to take our two gunships on a long flight to an Army artillery support base north of Saigon at a place called Chu Chi, to support a big amphibious river assault operation. After we landed at the strange new airfield on a large Army base, I asked one of the line crew who I needed to talk to get fuel and ammo and berthing for my guys. He told me I had to talk to "Top." I asked him who this Top guy was and he pointed to the headquarters building with the tall flag pole across the runway and said that was where I would find this guy named Top. He was grinning when I said the word, Top. I crossed the runway and walked in the office, only to find a beautiful air-conditioned mahogany paneled office with an Army sergeant, sitting at a desk. I asked if he was "Top"— he looked me up and down with a cold stare. Now, I'm in a sweaty old flight-suit, a Navy ball cap on my head and needed a haircut and a shave. He looked at me for a full minute before he told me to wait there, right where I was standing. He went through a door behind him, came out, and waited another full minute before he stated to me that Top would see me and I could go in. I walked into the office and there sat "Top" at his big desk, in a starched uniform, with plaques and flags on the mahogany walls and a big brass name plate on his desk that read "First Sergeant" – that's when I realized who "Top" was.

I was just a new Lieutenant (Junior Grade) with zero horsepower in front of a grizzled old E-9, but I gave him my whole story and he just looked at me with a blank stare, shaking his head. He finally gave me a grin as he picked up the phone, telling whoever answered to give those Navy helo guys whatever they needed. After thanking him and inviting him to go for a ride with us, I made it back to the flight-line in time to see a pick-up, a fuel truck, and a van arriving at the aircraft with whatever we needed. Welcome to the Army!

After I returned home from Vietnam, I received orders to report to HS-4 Helicopter Anti-Submarine Squadron 4 in San Diego flying a Sikorsky Sea King (H-3) in the ASW (Anti-Submarine Warfare) role.

My squadron soon deployed to WestPac (Western Pacific) on USS *Ticonderoga* (CV-14), the sister-ship to Yorktown, in late 1970. One incident stands out in my mind during that cruise. I was flying on a late night ASW patrol in the South China Sea off the Chinese coast near Hainan Island, about 100 miles from the ship. Out of complete boredom, my copilot started playing around with the aircraft ARN-25 radio, which was capable of picking up commercial radio stations. We were searching through frequencies listening to Chinese music broadcasts when all of a sudden my copilot said, "Hey, I think they are talking about us!" – I looked at him and said rather sarcastically, "Sure they are!" He held up his hand for me to be quiet and I watched his eyes get wide – he looked at me and, in a serious voice, said, "They're talking about a helicopter on radar and I think it's us!" he replied, "How in the hell do you know that?" He said he understood Chinese because he was a Mormon, and was sent on a mission to Taiwan, when he was in college, and learned to speak the language. I thought he was just pulling my leg and I called it BS; however, he insisted he was being honest and he really looked scared.

He listened for a while and said "Hey, I hear something about us being in their area and something about missiles or rockets" That was enough for me. I said, "OK, that's enough for me," and we turned around and headed back to the ship as low and as fast as we could go. When we got back and debriefed the flight, my copilot turned out to be the only Chinese linguist in the whole battle group! He never thought it was important to tell anyone that he understood Chinese, and needless to say, he was scooped up by the Intel' folks and his flying days were done for a while. (Battle Group couldn't afford to lose that valuable asset!).

Following that tour in HS-4, I was assigned as an instructor pilot in HS-10 flying the H-3. During that tour I was assigned to train several Iranian helo pilots who had been sent to San Diego from the Shah's Royal Air Force for flight training in the H-3. The majority of the pilots had some experience, and they were pretty good, as long as we flew in daylight conditions with no bad weather. Night and instrument flying was a different story. After shore duty tour as instructor pilot, I returned to HS-4 and deployed again to WestPac on USS *Kitty Hawk* in 1976.

We were about a week out of Subic Bay on the transit to WestPac when the ship suffered a major emergency, with a serious fire and explosion in one of the main engine rooms. The smoke from the burning oil got sucked into the ship's air conditioning system and quickly filled the ship with clouds of thick black smoke. It was about 2100 and we were just finishing up a card game in the ready room when the toxic smoke started pouring out of the overhead vents. In seconds the ship sounded "General Quarters" "General Quarters - this is not a drill!" Our ready room was just below the flight deck and when we scrambled out the hatch and up the ladder we saw dozens of other sailors already pouring out of the ship. The fire was finally brought under control but the ship went dead in the water for about twenty-four hours with all systems secured. Food and water were brought up to the crew who chose to stay on the flight deck. The sailors carried their mattresses out to the open flight deck, where we slept under the stars for two nights, sweating profusely in the tropical heat, dining on C-rats, while the carrier rolled like an empty beer can in the Pacific Ocean swell. The ship finally made it to Subic Bay, Philippines, and went cold iron for about six weeks while the damage was repaired. Unfortunately, the ship lost six sailors in the engine room fire. After the ship was repaired we departed for the Indian Ocean as the first carrier battle group to deploy to that area. That deployment lasted eleven months. Port visits in Pearl Harbor, Cubi Point, Shang Hi, Siri Lanka and Diego Garcia, and were highlights of that deployment.

Following deployment on *Kitty Hawk* and returning to San Diego, I was looking for a new challenge and requested transition to fly the LAMPS (Light Airborne Multi-Purpose) missions in the Kaman Seasprite (H-2) from the deck of destroyers. After finally getting approval to make the change, I went through H-2 flight training and was assigned to HSL-35 in San Diego. After receiving and training my crew, we deployed again to WestPac, on USS *Reasoner* (FF-1063), a fast frigate, where I was the Officer-in-Charge of the helicopter detachment. The ship was ordered to make a single ship transit from San Diego to Japan via Pearl Harbor. When the ship was approaching Japan and about 300 miles from the island of Iwo Jima, we received a mayday distress call from a Coast Guard Loran station on the island for two missing sailors in a small boat. The ship proceeded at flank speed to close on the island and we launched the helo on a SAR (Search & Rescue) mission to search for the missing men. We eventually found them alive and beached on the far side of the island in an overturned boat. We landed on the beach and picked them up to return them to their station. Interesting side of this story is that we saw Iwo Jima up close –- flew over the top of Mt Surabachi, saw old gun emplacements, pill boxes, old tanks and vehicles of all description still rusting in the sand – and the Japanese Rising Sun still visible, painted on the roof of a rusty old hanger. While we were on the beach picking up the stranded sailors, one of my crewmen managed to scoop up some black volcanic sand from the beach. When we got back to the ship the XO carefully divided up the sand and gave every sailor a small pill bottle with a few grains from the *"Sands of Iwo Jima!"*

Later in the deployment, we were assigned to accompany the USS *Oklahoma City* (CG-5) (last WWII heavy cruiser still on active duty) on her final cruise through the South Pacific with the Seventh Fleet Commander aboard. We made port calls in Rabal, New Guinea, Sydney, Australia, Hobart, Tasmania (yes - Tasmania! - some great stories), Bunbury, Australia, Hong Kong and Singapore. Well, maybe a few we can publish. Here goes:

CRUISE THROUGH THE SOUTH PACIFIC WITH A PORT VISIT TO HOBART, TASMANIA! 1977!

Following the dramatic rescue of the two lost Coast Guard sailors on the island of Iwo Jima, the USS *Reasoner* proceeded to Atsugi, Japan, where she reported to Commander, Seventh Fleet for further assignment. While waiting our next orders, rumors were flying through the ship as to where we would go next, with everyone having their own ideas and taking side bets on which were the favored ports. Early one morning a messenger arrived at the ship with a briefcase tightly gripped in his hand, asking to see the Captain of the ship right away. The Captain was called to his cabin to meet the messenger and within a few minutes the whole ship was buzzing with excitement.

The messenger left the ship after his meeting with the Captain and the rumor mill started working overtime, with everyone offering their own opinion as to where we were headed next. Nothing was heard from the "head office" the rest of the day, but after the evening meal the Captain finally came on the ship's public address system. He announced that our ship had been selected to accompany the US Ambassador to Australia and the Seventh Fleet Admiral on his flagship the USS *Oklahoma City*, one of the last of the WWII heavy cruisers, for a final tour through the South Pacific to show the flag. The *Oklahoma City* was scheduled to be retired from service following this cruise and she was very revered by the Australians for her service in the war.

The USS *Reasoner*, with the LAMPS helicopter detachment aboard, was to accompany the *Oklahoma City* to provide helicopter transportation and logistics services. Needless to say, everyone on the ship was cheering and high-fiveing, really excited about the prospects of the voyage. After a few days of intense resupply the ships were finally ready to depart. The officers and chiefs on the ship were directed to procure rarely worn and special Tropical White Short uniforms for the State visits expected along the way. (White shirt, white shorts with white knee-high socks and shoes - and white pith helmets).

We departed Japan on schedule and proceeded south towards the equator, with great anticipation by all the "pollywogs" on the ship for "crossing the line" ceremonies that were soon to befall us. In the ancient tradition of mariners, crossing the equator at sea turns a sailor from a lowly Pollywog into a seasoned Shellback, with a ceremony on the ship that only one who has experienced it can begin to appreciate - or talk about! Needless to say, we all survived to tell the tale, receiving our hard won certificates as duly indoctrinated Shellbacks into King Neptune's Kingdom.

First port call of the trip was in Rabaul, Papua New Guinea. Rabaul is a town on the island of New Britain in the Solomon Sea. It lies inside of a huge ancient volcanic crater, one side of which had collapsed into the sea eons ago, leaving a passage from the ocean into a deep lagoon of the most beautiful turquoise blue water, surrounded by high mountains covered in coconut palms and tropical jungle growth. After tying up at the town pier, we were escorted by the local military and government officials to a reception at a beautiful old French plantation home in town that looked like it was straight out of an old Humphrey Bogart movie. We were told that during WWII, the Japanese had occupied the area, and had excavated large caves in the side of the volcano walls where they hid submarines, some of which were reported to be still in the caves, abandoned after the war.

Departing Rabaul, we proceeded through the Solomon Sea, stopping at Bougainville and Guadalcanal islands to lay wreaths in honor of the US forces lost there in the epic battles of the war in the Pacific. We received word that the USS *Oklahoma City*, with the Commander Seventh Fleet and Australian Ambassador aboard, would be making port visits in Sydney and Melborne, but the USS *Reasoner* would not be accompanying them. Instead, we received orders to proceed to Hobart, Tasmania, for a week's port visit! We also learned that we would be the first US Navy ship to visit Hobart in many years. (Tasmania is an island south of the Australian continent. Hobart is the capital city of the island nation state).

Excitement spread throughout the ship, and all hands turned out to sweep, clean, dust and polish her from stem to stern for the port visit. During the trip south we received a message from the advance shore party in Hobart that the town had put out a "dial-a-sailor" wish list for any citizen who wanted to host a sailor for a meal, a sightseeing trip or an overnight. The total compliment of officers and men aboard the *Reasoner* numbered about 360 men - by the time the ship arrived the "dial-a-sailor" request line had over 700 requests to host a sailor to do something! The day the ship arrived, the Lord Mayor of Hobart declared a holiday, and the entire town greeted us on the pier at foot of Hobart's main street - with a brass band playing and flags flying. After the ship was secured and all the sailors had time to put on their best uniforms, the ship was opened for visitors. As the guests came aboard and walked around the ship they were handing each sailor a small business card with their name and number, offering to host them while we were in port. By the time the open house was over, every sailor on the ship had several invitations in their pockets.

As the week went on, the normal duty watches were set on ship, but sailors not on duty were encouraged to go ashore with people who had invited them as their guests. Every man on the ship was in high demand and the food and beverages were in ample supply everywhere we went. There was hardly time to sleep, and everyone was soon exhausted from the hectic schedule. The people of Hobart were very warm, generous, and welcoming, and very excited to have a bunch of "Yank sailors" in their town. The ship's store sold out of ships hats, t-shirts and pins by the second day.

Our day of departure finally arrived and the ship was busy getting ready to get underway. As our departure time approached, people started gathering at the dock to see us off. Soon the entire town had gathered, waving and wishing us well, and the sailors on *Reasoner* were lining the rails waving and shouting back to the crowd. Everyone had had a great experience and made many new friends, and there were even a few new budding romances among the crew. Someone on the ship had gotten a tape recording of the song "*Waltzing Matilda*" - and it started playing over the loud speakers as the ship was backing away from the dock. Among the cheering and waving crowd, there was more than one person wiping their eyes as we pulled away.

Hobart is located about six miles up a river from the ocean. As the ship turned into the stream and the watches were set, the Captain came on the ship's public address. He said something like …. "Men, this is the Captain speaking. I have been in the Navy over thirty years and have never had a port visit like this one. If you are not on duty, you are secured - everyone hit the rack and get some sleep!" A collective cheer could be heard throughout the ship as everyone was completely exhausted after a very memorial week in Tasmania.

The next port we hit was Bunbury, on the western coast of the Australian continent. The weather on our arrival was dismal - wind and rain were pelting the ship and the harbor was full of whitecaps. We didn't get tied up and secured until well after dark, so everyone stayed aboard until the next day. The morning broke sunny and bright, but still with a stiff wind blowing. We were tied up at a commercial wharf in a shipyard so the throngs of welcomers were not there, but there was a line of taxi cabs waiting to take us "downtown" as soon as we were off the ship. Bunbury and the people reminded us of what the US might have looked like in an earlier era - almost like the wild-west. The people were just as welcoming and excited to have a US Navy ship in town, but they were more rugged in appearance and manner. Many beat-up old pickup trucks, cowboy hats, boots and jeans were seen on the streets, and all the pubs were separated into two sections - men on one side, women on the other. Every pub had an ongoing dart game, with money wagers on every throw of the dart. Every pub we went in we were immediately challenged to a game of darts. The restaurants were modest but with excellent food and plenty of cold beer. While I was on a sightseeing drive with a local family to see the kangaroos, we came across a hand-lettered sign nailed to a gate leading up a dirt road. It said "no sneaky beaks allowed!" - I asked my hosts what that meant and they all had a good laugh - explaining that it was the same thing as our version of sticking your nose into someone's business!!

A visit to Singapore was next on the list where we rejoined the *Oklahoma City*. We spent several days being hosted by local government officials to tours of the city, picnics and sports matches for the crew and several lavish parties for the officers and chiefs. That's where we all got to wear our special Tropical White Short uniforms.

Hong Kong was next on the agenda. The most memorable event of that port visit was an invitation from the Australian aircraft carrier HMS *Melborne*, which happened to be in port at the same time. We were touring the city and stopped for lunch where we meet some of guys from the helo squadron on the *Melbourne*. They immediately invited us to be their guests that evening for what they called a "jolly good piss-up" - what we called a beer bust or kegger - at the famous Hong Kong China Fleet Club. We spent several hours drinking beer, eating great food, telling stories and singing bawdy sea ballads with our new Aussie mates. A great time was had by all - at least that's what I remember! We pulled out of Hong Kong the next day and proceeded to Subic Bay in the Philippines to end the most memorable cruise I have ever had the pleasure of experiencing.

After returning to San Diego, I was ordered to HSL-31, the H-2 training squadron, as a flight Instructor, when I was offered the opportunity to deploy again as the Officer-in-Charge of a utility helicopter detachment onboard the oceanographic research vessel USNS Chauvenet (TAGS-29). After gathering and training my crew, we all flew commercial to Cebu City in the Philippines, where we met the ship and immediately departed to the south for the Makassar Straits, a body of water between Borneo and the Celebes Islands and a major shipping lane, to conduct ocean bottom topography mapping for the Navy. For six months we flew logistics support for the ship and deployed ground crews on many small coral islands in the area. I landed on many remote uninhabited beaches, and visited with natives in small villages who had never seen an American or a helicopter before. They were suspicious but curious about us, and we were able to communicate with the help of Indonesian Naval officers who traveled with us. On one very memorable flight, I flew over and down into the crater of the Krakatoa Volcano on Sumatra. That's the volcano that erupted in 1883 with world-wide cataclysmic results. It was like flying in a movie set of the series *Star Wars*, pretty scary but it was an experience I will never forget.

Following that tour I was ordered to Pearl Harbor, Hawaii on the staff of CINCPACFLT (Commander-In-Chief, Pacific Fleet) as the Operations Briefing Officer. I briefed the CINC and his staff every morning for the next three years, and was on duty when a Soviet Su-15 Interceptor shot down Korean airliner KAL-007, a Boeing-747, over the Sea of Japan killing all aboard.

This incident severely raised tensions between the USSR and the United States. We spent the next two weeks locked up in the command center, with my wife bringing me clean uniforms every few days!

After Hawaii, I received orders to attend the National War College at Ft McNair, in Washington, DC. Following a year of study in national and international policies and politics, I received orders to the Naval War College in Newport, RI. I was on the faculty, teaching in the naval operations and war gaming departments, and was a sponsor for several foreign officers attending the College. I retired following that tour and went into the real estate business for the next 25 years.

That's kinda it.

You got some more . . . don't you?

Oh, maybe there are a couple more events I'd like to tell you about:

Go for it, Paul.

You asked for it. Here goes:

MAIL DELIVERY TO USCG SHIP

Our helo detachment was stationed at the mouth of the Song Ong Doc River where it flows into the Gulf of Thailand. The terrain both north and south of us was largely coastal forest and open rice paddies, interspaced by small canals and rivers flowing to the sea. The area was known to be favored by the Viet Cong and NVA as an infiltration route for supplies to their forces further south in the Mekong Delta.

Navy destroyers would frequently appear off the coast near us to provide gun-fire support to the US and ARVN ground forces patrolling the area, especially the U-Minh Forest, which was a dense jungle area particularly favored by the VC. They conducted H and I fire (harassment and interdiction) along the coastal Viet Cong infiltration transit routes. One day we received a message that a new Coast Guard cutter was going to be on station for gun-fire support and they we would be tasked to provide just that. None of us had seen one of the new high endurance cutters and we were excited about our new visitor. We communicated with them via radio for several weeks, calling gun-fire missions and enemy troop movements, but never had a chance to visit the ship or even see her close up. One day we had a logistics helo from the home squadron arrive at our pad with a big load of mail for the Coast Guard ship. We called the ship and told them what we had and they asked if we could deliver it to them. Since we did not have hoists on our helicopters, it meant we would have to land on their small flight deck to drop off the mail. My crew was the next up to fly on the schedule so I got the mission for the delivery. As we flew out over the coast to meet the ship and as we got closer we could see that she was a sparkling white high endurance cutter named the USCG *Morganthau* (WHEC-732). We arrived over the ship and started our approach to the deck - the first thing I remember seeing is all the flight deck personnel were in CLEAN, PRESSED dungarees with new yellow flight deck vests still showing box creases. We landed and shut down and I think every sailor on the ship came on the flight deck eager to look at our helo and see what we looked like. We lived in a pretty austere environment on the beach, took showers rarely and only washed our flight suits when it rained. Combined with smelling like sweat, JP-4 fuel and hydraulic fluid, with scruffy beards and shaggy hair, we musta presented quite a sight to the Coasties! We were greeted on the flight deck by the CO who asked if we could stay for lunch and I said we would be honored to join them. The CO then asked if we would like to "clean up" before lunch as he gave me the once over - I looked at his crisp starched uniform and all the sailors standing around us that were in clean, creased dungarees and quickly got the message. I eagerly accepted and my copilot and I and my two crewmen were escorted into the ship and down to the crews berthing area. We took off our flight suits and stepped into the first hot water showers we had had in a very long time. After drying off and being provided clean jumpsuits we were given razors to shave and got haircuts from the barber right there on the mess decks! We were treated like heroes by the crew and had a terrific lunch with real cooked food for a great treat! We were used to eating our meals out of a box or can (C-rats!) so sitting down to a real hot meal was a special event. After lunch the XO came in and handed us our flight suits - they had been washed and dried by the ship's laundry while we were eating. We then got a tour of the ship by the XO, ending up on the bridge where we were treated to a full power run of the ship - zero to thirty knots in sixty seconds with twin turbine engines! When we were on the deck ready for takeoff for departure, the whole crew was lining the rails waving to us - we all felt like heroes! After arriving back to our detachment at Song Ong Doc, later that day all the guys that had stayed behind wouldn't get anywhere close to us because they said we all smelled like soap and looked like politicians!

Post Script: The *Morganthau* was on her first deployment after being commissioned and was on her first patrol in Viet Nam when we landed aboard her. The crew had been off the coast of Viet Nam for over a month and only saw the war on the horizon from several miles off shore. When we landed on her deck we brought the real war to the crew of the ship, and for the first time they could see what that looked like in person. Looking back on the experience, I must admit that we looked pretty rough to the crew of the ship and understand why the CO asked us to "clean up our act" before joining them for lunch!

The *Morganthau* was finally retired in 2017 and was sold to Vietnam where she is still serving as a coastal patrol vessel with the Vietnamese Coast Guard. Interesting full circle twist to the story.

ATTACK ON VC BASE CAMP

One day I was called upon to see the Ops Officer at the home squadron. Walking into his office I was introduced to two guys in civilian clothes. (I immediately started thinking about "what did I do now?") The Ops Boss said they had something to talk to me about and what they had to say was to be considered confidential. They were CIA agents planning an operation to take out a major Viet Cong headquarters base that had been discovered in an area of the Mekong Delta called the U-Minh Forest. The enemy base camp was buried deep in the rain forest covered by a thick jungle canopy reaching 130' above the ground, which was almost impossible to penetrate with any ordinance that we had available at the time. I had been assigned by the Ops Boss to be the FTL (fire team leader) on a mission that was going to attempt to penetrate the jungle canopy to hit the VC camp from the air. The weapon of choice was going to be a cargo net full of 55 gallon barrels filled with gasoline, sling loaded under an Army CH-46 Chinook helicopter. I was to follow the Chinook into the target drop zone with two gunships, all guns loaded with belts of tracer ammo and "willy-pete" rockets (white phosphorus) - great for starting fires. The plan was for the Chinook, as it came over the target at a high altitude, to release the cargo net allowing the barrels to fall onto the trees below, hopefully bursting on impact. My job was to roll in and shoot everything I had into the trees where the barrels had fallen, in an attempt to ignite a massive blaze over the enemy base camp. We took off and proceeded on the mission, arriving over the suspected target area as planned. The Chinook released the barrels and I followed them down as they fell into the tree canopy, shooting at them as they hit the trees. One white phosphorus rocket hit the top of a tree and exploded just as a barrel burst open. I saw the fire erupt as we pulled off over the site, and turning back we saw the jungle canopy light up with red flames and black smoke pouring out of the trees. With great excitement we headed back to our base to meet up with the Army pilots and the civilian planners of the event. Because of our success, another mission was immediately planned for the next day, this time with more 55 gallon barrels than before. We arrived over the target as scheduled, the barrels were released, and both of our helos poured every round of ammo we had into the jungle canopy as the barrels descended into the trees. No smoke, no fire, no nothing. We made four more attempts in subsequent days to duplicate our first success but were never able to get the gas bombs to ignite. What we probably did was to provide the VC with hundreds of gallons of badly needed gasoline that literally fell from the skies above them. What must they have thought??

Research after that experience revealed that the use of "barrel bombs" had been tried previously in other areas of Viet Nam. The attempts had produced largely the same results as I experienced, with a massive forest fire that died quickly after the fuel was consumed, with little damage to enemy forces.

THE STORY OF FATHER MCNAMARA

Our small Seawolf detachment of 16 hardy sailors and two Huey helicopter gunships was stationed deep in the Mekong Delta far from our home squadron in Binh Thuy to the north. Our compound and landing pad were built on stilts over a mud flat close to a small coastal Vietnamese fishing village where the Song Ong Doc River flowed into the Gulf of Thailand. We had limited contact with our home squadron by HF radio and an occasional visit by a supply helo that would bring us aircraft parts, food, ammo and (sometimes) warm beer. In between we survived mostly on C-Rats and rain water in between supply drops. Our mission was to provide helicopter gunship cover for the PBR's and Swift boats that operated out of the floating support base across the river from us.

Every few weeks we would receive a message that we would be getting a visit from the "Holy Helo" - a helicopter bringing a Navy Chaplin down from the home guard, to hold a service and provide us an opportunity to worship. Our very favorite Chaplin was Father McNamara, known throughout the Delta as Father Mac. He was a fiery little Irishman from Boston with a great Irish brogue, red hair and beard and could relate to the guys like nobody I ever saw before.

The helo arrived early in the morning the next day and Father Mac set up a small alter on the helo pad with his religious vestments, candles and a bible for the service. We made benches with boards laid over ammo cans and the service was begun. After a few minutes we noticed the villagers were gathering, watching quietly from the fence. After the service was over, Father Mac walked over to the where the villagers were standing and greeted them in Vietnamese, and then he spoke to them in French. Several of the older villagers looked at him with a big smile and answered back - in French! Father Mac knew the older villagers had probably been around when the French occupied the country and had learned to speak the language.

After some back and forth between the village chief and Father Mac in French he told us we had been invited by the chief to join in a communal meal with the village - a rare and unusual event.

The meal was held that night in the center of the village under a large canopy of woven palm fronds, with the village chief and elders seated on mats on one side of the circle and Father Mac and all the Seawolves on the other side. Women and children were seated behind us in a circle. The food was brought out in a huge communal bowl - it looked like a broth or soup of some sort, with vegetables and fish, steaming hot, with a huge bowl of rice. The food was dipped from the big bowl into smaller bowls of carved wood by the women and passed around in the circle. When everyone had been served Father Mac offered a short prayer, but he said it in French, much to the delight of the older village members. That started an animated conversation around the circle, with Father Mac being the interpreter.

Soon after the meal was finished and cleared away, a large bowl filled with a milky white liquid was produced and placed in the center of our circle. The village chief dipped a small cup into the liquid and presented it to Father Mac who thanked him and drank it down. The cup was filled and passed to the next person in the circle, and so on-around, as was the local custom. We were drinking a local beverage made from fermented rice that was called something like "Ba-sa-de", and as I recall, tasted like chalk but had a pretty good kick. As the cup continued around the circle, the bowl was soon refilled and the conversation became more and more animated, with French, English and Vietnamese all mixing together. I remember Father Mac starting to sing the old French melody *Frere Jacques*, and soon everyone was singing verse after verse at the top of their lungs. Even the kids were singing as loud as they could.

The rest of the evening remains a little hazy after all this time, but I remember that we finally ended up carrying Father Mac back to our compound and pouring his holy-self into a spare bunk to sleep it off. The next day we were all feeling the effects of the night before, but we got Father Mac up early, and after a few cups of coffee he did another short service for the guys before his helo arrived to take him back to the home squadron. It was a great experience for all of us and one of my fondest memories of my time in country.

Let's talk about your after the war and Navy life. Where were you in real estate?

Newport, RI

Paul, were you married?

First marriage ended shortly after I returned from Viet Nam, for all the unfortunate reasons that many other returning vets experienced at that particular time. My first real job out of the Navy in 1994 was as a Harbormaster on Block Island, RI, a small island off the coast of Rhode Island and Connecticut. I stayed a year in the job but decided that wasn't where I wanted to spend my retirement years, so I moved back to Newport and decided to study for a real estate license. I met my current wife Patricia, who was also in the real estate business, shortly after I started to work. We eventually became a husband/wife team and worked together for the next fifteen years, owning our own brokerage for the last few years of business. We first came to Charleston for a squadron reunion in 2012, fell love with the charm of the low country, and decided to move permanently shortly thereafter.

What caused you to become a volunteer at Patriots Point?

I was looking for a way to volunteer in my new community, and I happen to run into Dick Livingston in a Publix supermarket parking lot. He had a blue Patriot's Point Volunteer shirt on and I asked him what that was all about. When he told me about the volunteer program, I was hooked! He gave me Dick West's email address and the rest is history.

What has been an experience that sticks in your mind while on duty as a volunteer at PP?

I have thought about my experiences at Patriots Point and one thing really stands out in my mind. I have been very impressed with the determination of visitors who come to see the ship that arrive with various forms of physical handicaps and special needs. I have helped people in wheelchairs and walkers, crutches, canes and mobility carts, people with knee and hip replacement parts and people who are quite elderly and have limited mobility. They all go bravely aboard the ship and come out smiling and proud of their accomplishment. I have escorted these visitors to the elevator and picked them up after their tour, and to a person each and every one has been delighted and moved by what they saw and experienced. It has been a rather humbling experience but one that has really inspired me to understand the importance of what we have offer to our guests.

Have you met or had contact with a significant visitor at PP?

Yes – let me tell you the *Laffey* story

The USS *Laffey* was badly damaged in the battle for Okinawa in 1945, and was returned to the US to be repaired at the Bremerton Navy shipyard in Washington. When the badly damaged ship finally arrived in port; the Navy opened the ship for public viewing for two weeks before repairs were started. The Navy estimated that approximately 60,000 people toured the ship during this time.

One day last summer I was driving the shuttle bus when an elderly couple got in and sat in the back seat. As we were driving down the pier, I greeted them and asked where they were from, and what brought them to Patriot's Point. The gentleman said they were from Seattle, Washington and had come to Charleston to see the USS *Laffey*. I asked him why specifically the *Laffey*, and he said "I'm eighty-six-years-old and I wanted to see the ship again before I die, so we came to see her". I asked if he had served onboard the ship, but he said no, but his father worked in the Navy shipyard in Bremerton when the Laffey was brought in for repairs. He was only ten-years-old when his father took him on the ship and he said he always remembered seeing the damage and destruction the ship suffered, and had never forgotten it throughout his whole life. He vowed to see the ship again "before I die or am too old to make the trip." The hair literally stood up on the back of my neck when I realized how significant this visitor was and how important it was to make sure his visit to the *Laffey* was done properly. I contacted Hal Rigby and Graves Wilson on the radio and had them meet me on the dock where I introduced them to our guests. They in turn contacted our Public Affairs office who had a photographer meet them at the ship for a taped interview, and then gave them a guided tour of the *Laffey*.

That was the end of Paul's story. His was an amazing life in the Navy. He is a very good story teller and writer. As I was preparing to send this book to the publisher, Paul and I were together at Patriots Point one day, and he related the following story. I had to print it:

There was a pilot on my detachment named Barney that hailed from a little town, way back in the hills of rural Tennessee. About every three weeks or so, or whenever, we were fortunate to have an actual mail-call, and Barney would get a shoebox-size package in the mail. It would be wrapped carefully in brown paper with lots of tape to keep it secure. He would set it aside to wait for a quiet time in the hooch when we were all gathered together, when he would bring out the package and open it ceremoniously. The box was filled with popcorn, but tucked inside was a pint sized bottle filled with a clear liquid, carefully sealed with more tape. Barney would open the bottle, take a long sniff, and a cautious sip. Then, he would declare, with a smile that it was a "good batch" - of genuine Moonshine from his grandfather's working still up in them thar hills! We would all grab our coffee cups and gather 'round as Barney poured each of us a small amount of his grandfather's finest brew. We sipped it slowly, and it burned like fire going down, but after a few minutes, it left a nice warm feeling in the belly. Indeed, it was good "stuff."

On one occasion, Barney opened his "care package" from home (the rest of us usually got cookies that had turned to crumbs or socks and underwear), unscrewed the cap, took a long sniff, and then a cautious, tentative sip - made a terrible face and announced that this was a "bad batch," and not fit to drink. We all watched in dismay, with empty coffee cups in our hands, and gastric juices flowing, as he poured the whole bottle down the drain, telling us in his slow southern-mountain drawl "that crap can make you go blind, or crazy, so I'm throwing it out!" We were disappointed. No, make that stunned!

Thanks, Paul. You have had amazing experiences. Thanks for relating them, and thanks for being a volunteer at this Maritime and Naval Museum.

CHAPTER 4

JACK LEBER: A PATRIOTS POINT VOLUNTEER

★★★

Jack Leber: Photo property of author

Well, where do I start? Let's just go to the beginning. I was born in Newark, New Jersey, and continued living there until my family moved to Maplewood, NJ, during my senior year in high school. I attended St. Benedict's Preparatory School in Newark, NJ. St. Benedict's Prep was established 150 years ago by Benedictine Monks and was an all-boys school. I graduated in 1960. Afterward, I earned a mechanical engineering degree in 1964 from Newark College of Engineering (now

New Jersey Institute of Technology) and started working at Hewlett-Packard (HP) one week later.

I met my wife, Joy, at a church dance and we were married in 1968 in Mountainside, NJ, and lived in Westfield, NJ, until we moved to Randolph, NJ in 1972 when two HP facilities merged near there.

I held many different management positions during my thirty-five-year career with Hewlett-Packard, ultimately attaining the general manager level. I was the "start-up guy" with the company which ultimately led to my assignment to the Far East. My introduction to Asia was a brief (three weeks) consulting assignment in 1986 in Taiwan. Looking back, this may have been a test to see how I would fare in a new environment.

Beginning in late 1988, we began eight wonderful years in Seoul, Korea. Let me briefly describe those years:

Our family moved to Seoul in October 1988, and for our first six-months we experienced what it's like to be an expatriate, or expat for short. I like to describe it as being an "***illiterate minority***." I say that because of the feeling one gets by not being able to read, write or understand the language and customs in a city of eleven million Koreans. We were like a small raft of Americans in a sea of "foreigners." Of course, we were actually the foreigners.

In 1994, I was assigned to a different task, this time working in Beijing, China, while commuting there from Seoul to establish a research & development and marketing center.

During those eight years, my wife and family came home each summer to our shore home on Long Beach Island, NJ. However, we traveled to different Asian countries over the Christmas and New Year holidays.

We returned to New Jersey from Korea in September 1996. After all our travels my opinion is: ***The United States of America is not the only place in the world to live, but it is the best place in the world to live.***

While in Korea, I was a vice president of the American Chamber of Commerce in Korea (AMCHAM) and participated in many lobbying efforts in Washington, DC to improve business conditions in Korea for American companies. Two of the key AMCHAM issues at the time were opening market opportunities to import American-made goods into Korea (at the time, the Korean perspective was exports were good but imports were bad), and the protection of intellectual property rights, especially for pharmaceuticals. Oh yes! I was also a School Board member at Seoul Foreign School, where our two sons attended elementary and high school.

After living and working for eight years in Asia and traveling around various countries and experiencing different cultures, my observation is that ***people around the world are more the same than different – and most of the differences are enjoyable.***

Another interesting sideline was for ten years (in the late 70s and 80s) before moving to Korea we had a partnership, JL Ventures, with another family to build houses on Long Beach Island, NJ. We purchased the land and had a contractor construct the homes for us. We lived in a new home each summer for almost ten years and either sold or rented it the following year. Looking for a new real estate opportunity, we traveled to Charleston in the mid-80s and fell in love with area, especially Wild Dunes, where we purchased property.

I retired from HP in 1999 after thirty-five-years with the company, and then partnered in two startup ventures before fully retiring in 2003. My wife and I moved to Mt. Pleasant, SC, that same year.

As previously mentioned, we have two sons, John and Jeff. Since graduating from George Washington University, John has worked for the World Bank. Now, as an investment officer, he and his family have been based in Manila, Philippines, for the last four years to work on projects throughout Asia. He and his wife, Louise, have two daughters, Isabelle and Emily. Our other son, Jeff attended Georgia Tech, where he received a degree in electrical engineering and also studied finance. Today he is a Certified Financial Planner and partner with Bridger Schill Wealth Management Group. Jeff and his wife, Ashley, have three boys, Landon, Brennen, and Odin, and live in the Philadelphia area.

When someone asks me what I do now that I'm retired, I reply by saying: ***Volunteering is my retirement job.***

Besides playing golf regularly, I have several other interests. One activity is with the LPGA (Ladies Professional Golf Association) at their tournaments. My brother, Jim, and I have been involved with the LPGA since the late 1990s and typically volunteer at four or five tournaments around the country each year. We also hosted a number of players over the years. I also volunteered for several men's golf tournaments, tennis tournaments, and other local events here in the Charleston area.

My interest in the Navy began as a kid because my father always took my brother and me to Armed Forces Day events and the Port of Newark whenever a ship was open for visits. Also, my father's four brothers were Veterans, three WWII and one Korean War Veteran, so I heard a lot of stories about their experiences. In 2014, at the invitation of the Korean government, I attended a week of ceremonies in Korea with my Uncle Bill to commemorate the sixty-fourth anniversary of the start of the Korean War. It was a very memorable occasion and the first time I returned to Korea since a visit in 2000.

Jack Leber (left): Photo property of author

When I a met a former Patriots Point volunteer coordinator at a social event back in 2007, I asked him if you had to be a veteran to be a volunteer. When he said no, I signed up immediately because I wanted to give my time and effort to a worthy cause. I like meeting and talking to people from all around the world, and especially chatting with the many military veterans working, visiting, and volunteering at this naval and maritime museum. I've learned a lot about history, especially WWII, and the military over the past ten years. I am also privileged to have met a number of Medal of Honor heroes, who participated in symposiums and special events on the ship over the years.

JACK LEBER: PHOTO PROPERTY OF AUTHOR

Two memorable encounters with visitors to the Yorktown stick in my mind. While talking to a man at the USS *Franklin* exhibit, he told me that his father was a crew member on the ship during the attack. Obviously, he survived and made his way back to Hawaii and then the Brooklyn Navy Yard where the major repairs were done. He said that's where he met his wife. If that attack didn't happen he would have never met that woman. In a second instance, a man and his wife asked me where the engine room is, and if it was open to visitors. I directed him to Tour #2 and after about an hour he returned to tell me that he had an eerie feeling that his father was still down there.

Stuff like that tends to make the hair on the back of the neck stand straight out.

My Patriots Point activities expanded over the last year to include teaching history to fifth-grade students from various schools in SC, leading tours for campers, and at night a guide for the Yorktown ghost tours. I am also a Navy League member and periodically attend some of their functions.

I'm proud to be a Patriots Point Volunteer.

Jack

CHAPTER 5
VOLUNTEER DICK AMEN

★★★

Dick Amen: Photo property of author

Dick Amen is a volunteer at Patriots Point Naval and Maritime Museum. This is his story:

I emerged into this world in the big city of New York, New York. My youthful development was associated with those surroundings as well as in Alexandria, Virginia, a suburb of Washington, DC, and in Pelham

Manor, NY, a suburb of New York City. My life was similar to an episode of *Leave it to Beaver* – a relatively normal suburban life. I graduated from Archbishop Stepinac High School in White Plains, NY, then, in 1963, attended Cornell School of Engineering for three semesters and went on to receive a Bachelor's degree in Business Administration from Manhattan College in 1968. My greatest pleasure during those years was playing high school and intercollegiate college football. After college I "enrolled" in Uncle Sam's boy's camp (the Army). After separation, I received a Master's Degree in Business Administration from Columbia University, 1973.

I was in my last year of college - 1968 - when news of the Vietnam War became a major tele-journalist subject every night. The famous TET Offensive was a major focus of almost all of the few TV newscasts. My intense feelings of empathy for our warriors in Vietnam (VN), and patriotism for our country, left me no alternative but to enlist: Duty, Honor, Country! Serving in the military during a war – in a warm climate - was on my bucket list. I couldn't imagine someone throwing a war and not inviting me! Lastly, I couldn't imagine going through life vulnerable to criticism for dodging the draft and/or my perceived duty. So I happily enlisted for Army Infantry Officer Candidate School. (OCS). I could never have imagined doing anything else.

There was also a limited family tradition. My dad was a communications officer on CV-17, the USS *Bunker Hill* in the Pacific during World War II and was aboard when it was crippled by two kamikaze planes. CV-17 was an Essex class carrier as was the *Yorktown*, (CV-10). Dad always thought I was nuts for volunteering for Army OCS. He used to tell me that a Navy officer had his own bunk, fresh hot chow, clean sheets, a head, etc. I told him I gave that much consideration, but in the final analysis, "I guess I can't swim as far as I can walk." I'm not sure he ever understood that I had to be closer to the "action," and in more control of my destiny. So, infantry, here I am. (Being on the Yorktown has been a very interesting contrast: we didn't have such big toys in the Army!)

I entered the Army in May of 1968. It was a volcanic culture shock: discipline, harassment, communal living, non-existence of privacy, etc. Somehow, I abandoned my very individualist and independent ways and got through those first months. I was selected as Soldier of the Cycle in my Fort Dix, NJ training company, ran second in my Advanced Infantry Training at Fort Polk, Louisiana and third Honor Graduate of my Officer Candidate School. I volunteered for Airborne (jump) School because it looked like fun and I would likely never have another chance to parachute under such favorable conditions. (Another item on my bucket list.) I nearly volunteered for Ranger School, but it didn't look like much fun.

Airborne school was a hoot. After six months in OCS, I was in prime physical condition. That made the physical demands much easier than for most other airborne students. It was more like a vacation after OCS. As officer trainees, it was like a nine-to-five job: training during the day and hard partying at night. It was very thorough and efficient over a three-week period. When jump week started, everyone was primed and ready for our five qualifying jumps. (On my first qualifying jump, the jumpmaster denied my exit, so we - a buddy of mine (Cliff Purcell) and I - had to land, get re-manifested and make a second attempt. The same thing almost happened again. The stick was slow in jumping and as we neared the end of the DZ, the jumpmaster started to lower his arm, attempting to block our exit. I pushed past him while Cliff hung on to my d-bag. We both went out of the plane, ass over tea kettle, and got tangled in the shroud lines. It was a little hairy for a moment, but training set-in for a happy ending. Unexpectedly, we landed just inside the drop zone and took a long hike to the pickup point. It was a hell of a first jump! Happily, we were so far out of sight that no one could identify us. It would have been a major kerfuffle.

After earning my jump wings, I was assigned as company XO of the 43rd Company, 4th Student Battalion, at Fort Benning, GA. We were affectionately known as "black hats" for the black baseball caps that were the uniform covers. What great duty for a newly commissioned office waiting for orders to Nam! Made lots of jumps; spent plenty of time at happy hour at the "O" club; lots of off duty time; lots of company barbecues with officer jump students and senior cadre of the company, skillfully arranged by one of the best mess sergeants in the Army: Sergeant First Class Fletcher. (Bless you Fletcher, where ever you are!) That duty remains as one of the most carefree times of my life: no job worries, no mortgage, no health insurance problems, no wardrobe concerns, etc. It was a singular joy! I met a clerk in the orders section who notified me about four months before I had to rotate to VN, well before the normal notice period. The emphasis on partying took a big uptick at that time. Given the mood of the moment, it wasn't hard to find opportunities for merry-making.

I was subsequently ordered to Panama for Jungle Warfare School before going overseas. It turned out to be another grown-up boy's camp: rappelling, zip-line riding, etc. next to the beach on the Caribbean Sea. A few field training exercises (FTXs) interrupted the fun and games, but all in all was it was a pleasant diversion. (I should note that, prior to departing for Panama, the base commander at the Charleston AFB arrested and confined almost all of my OCS classmates for a little too much partying, about thirty or so of us; however, nothing too extreme. It was another opportunity to party with other GI's awaiting VN rotation, and party we did! No one cared about boundaries. What are you going to do, send me to Vietnam? The commander was really cross. I think he was yanked out of bed, around one or two am. We were confined on the MAT flight, six or eight hours before the scheduled flight time. He swore that this was the only time any troops were so disciplined and that, if we all weren't headed for VN, there would have been some serious charges. (I certainly have fond memories of that night, but can't recount them here. Sorry!)

After that it was a few more weeks of leave, and then a less than pleasant flight to VN on a MAT - Military Airlift Command, I think - charter.

I finally arrived in the land of the land of "cool water buffalo." After a short indoctrination and a brief language course, I was assigned to an advisory team. Officially, I was no longer a part of the US Army. We got no direct support from Uncle Sam. NONE! (We were a true charity case!) It was nearly impossible to get quick dust-off rescue choppers; no artillery or air support. We were really on our own. No one had the responsibility to keep us re-supplied, so pretty much all of our food and supplies were either purchased on the local market or scrounged from other US Units. In recognition of our orphaned status, we were given a subsistence allowance for local food purchases. I don't think many GI's were so treated. I was the teams scrounge and had many adventures trying to barter for supplies. Sometimes, I would trade VC (Viet Cong) flags, made by some local women for the team. It was usually good for a case of steaks at the Signal base at Phu Lam and other rear area bases.

On the bright side, I was pretty much on my own. I doubt anyone really knew where I was on any given day. I'm not sure I knew where I was on any given day! There were few signs in the bush and no road maps. It worked out great for me not having any REMF [rear echelon mother f*****] second guessing my operations and commands. I don't know of any second lieutenant that had so much unsupervised command latitude.

At that time, 1969 and 1970, the military was downsizing its operational units and exiting Vietnam during the process of "Vietnamization." Vietnamization, was the plan to have Vietnamese units take over as US forces rotated back to "the land of the big PX." Since the Vietnamese weren't ready to take responsibility, small Special-Forces-type teams were hastily organized to shore up the Vietnamese units and to independently act as "force multipliers," a job normally associated with "Green Beenies." As usual for the Army, when the supply of a needed MOS (military occupational specialty) was less than demand, standards were re-established. New MOSs were created. Training moved to an over-balance of on-the-job training. You got your feet wet and learned as you went along.

"My job in 'Nam was quite unique. I commanded a team of five GIs: two officers, two senior infantry NCOs and a medic. We were never assigned to any regular US Army unit, but deployed to different elements of Vietnamese armed forces. My team worked most often with Regional Force units (RF/PF), some Korean units (ROKs), and some anti-communist guerillas: the People's Self Defense Force (PSDF). We wore Vietnamese insignias in addition to US Army and drove VN designated vehicles. My chain of command was one level below a civilian in Saigon. I had virtually no on-site, minute to minute chain-of command supervision. Usually, we were out of radio, artillery and/or gunship range. I often flew Air America (operated by the C.I.A.), but that is a different story. I pretty much ran my own private war, with the exception of numerous formal briefings to bird colonels and brigadier generals.

My initial mission concentrated on interdicting the supply routes coming from the Ho Chi Minh Trail through the Parrots Beak (the prominent triangular extension of Cambodia into Vietnam northwest of Saigon) into Saigon. We were stationed in a forward operating base that was about half way between Saigon and the tip of the beak, and somewhat south of Cu Chi and the "Black Virgin Mountain" – Nui Ba Den. We were to interdict Vet Cong and NVA and their supplies going into this area and the capital. Normal operations were search and destroy missions and night ambushes as well as almost nightly helicopter Night Hawk missions. During a Night Hawk mission, a bait helo with search light, would fly low and slow to attract enemy gunfire. Helicopter gunships or Cobras (heavily armed attack choppers) flying high cover would respond to targeted flares and/or smoke to fire for effect. It worked great as long as "Charlie" missed the bait bird and me. Not everyone was so "lucky."

Later in my tour, I developed and ran a program of basic military training and execution for the PSDF, some of which were undoubtedly VC. (I used to sleep with one eye opened during that part of my mission. Some of my cadre trainees and "students" were not so diligent and less fortunate, and were KIA'd in their sleep.) Anyway, it contributed to the pacification of the area.

At this point, let Dick's continuing story be told from an interview contained in the Winter 2014 Edition of "SCUTTLEBUTT" @ PatriotsPoint.org, with permission from the Scuttlebutt editor and chapter author:

Not unexpectedly, Dick has many stories, but not many that he's willing to share with people. However, here is one that he's willing to tell. *"On my first deployment to a remote ARVN fire base, I was invited to meet the camp commander. Naturally, as senior officer I was obliged to accept and engage in rapport-building exercises. I met with the commander and four or five of his staff in a small bunker. After introductions, we sat at a picnic table where I was offered a shot of Johnnie Walker Red from a communal shot glass and some cooked duck from a communal dish. Neither could be refused; although I really figured I'd die of food poisoning by dawn (I nearly did!). So I dutifully had a shot of the Johnny Walker Red and took a piece of the diced duck with all the bones still in place. I hadn't expected that the tidbit had more bones than meat, but I chewed the hell out of it. Nowhere were there dishes or napkins, so I did the only thing I could think of: I swallowed the whole damn mess! Round after round, tidbit after tidbit, and the action was repeated until the bottle was dry and the duck was finished. At that point, I must have had a ton of duck bones growling in my stomach. I couldn't believe that the ARVN's weren't equally distressed. However, when we all got up to leave and bid farewell, an old lady (ba mop) came in to clean up. It was then that I noted there were piles of bones around the tables under the seats of the others. Unbeknownst to me, they were chewing the bony duck and, when my attention was diverted, would spit them into their hands and toss them under the picnic tables at which we sat. It was not polite to see a quest spit out anything, but apparently okay to* *watch him swallow duck bones. Well, I guess they thought that I was really strange, but accepted me and my behavior."*

On another occasion, I was the focus of a number of Vietnamese soldiers wanting a drinking bout at a local village chief's home. Each soldier would make a toast with me individually and then pass me off to the next. I was putting down 4 or 5 shots of bac si dai (Vietnamese rice wine) vs the bunch of them. Worse still, they were dipping their shot glasses in a tumbler full of water, and I had the real thing – indistinguishable to the naked eye from the sake like liquid I was consuming. They were out to get me loaded and were succeeding very nicely, indeed. My senior NCO: SFC Sprouse, called their bluff and drank them under the table, as the expression goes. Sadly for Sprouse, he passed out and was unconscious for a bit more of that 36 hours. (I think his hangover lasted for a week!)

Dick left the Army in 1971 as a first lieutenant. He was awarded the Bronze Star, ARCOM Combat Infantry Badge, Airborne wings, Air Medal (awarded to very few infantrymen), the Vietnamese Cross of Gallantry with bronze cluster and the Vietnamese Medal of Honor (very rarely bestowed). Unfortunately, Dick left the Army with a very bad case of hepatitis from eating and drinking local food. Therefore, he convalesced for a while. Dick recalls that, "it took several years to fully recover from the hepatitis." Dick went to grad school and received a Master's in Business Administration from Columbia University in 1973.

Most of my civilian career was involved, one way or the other, in international mergers and acquisitions. In some respects, it was similar to Airborne warfare. I would "drop" into any number of foreign and domestic locales, usually alone to recon the area and situation and conduct my "mission." (To paraphrase some lines from "Band of Brothers," Sergeant says: "Sir, you're going to be surrounded!" Captain says:

"Sergeant, we're Airborne! We were supposed to be surrounded!") Once again, I was substantially unsupervised and on my own. Happily, my batting average in pursuing and completing multi-million dollar transactions was good enough to become one of the youngest Vice Presidents at Revlon. It was a great company; great people; and a singular opportunity for one with strong autonomous, independent - and somewhat arrogant – personality. I also worked in financial management at Seagram and Sons, Gulf & Western in New York City and several private investment banks. I finished my career as a real estate investor and broker on Long Island, NY. I guess I was still operating on my own when I retired from corporate in 1989 and retired to boating and fishing in the Atlantic, south of Long Island. I moved to Mt. Pleasant in November 2011. Actually, I followed my older daughter to Charleston. I had also experienced an earth quake, a flood, a hurricane and the near collapse of the local real estate market. Talk about a sign from the gods!! I am presently unemployed, searching for a new career. I am way too bored to sit on my butt and watch the sunset.

Dick is divorced and has two daughters. One has graduated from College of Charleston and one will soon graduate from the University of South Carolina in Columbia, SC.

His special interests include furniture and cabinet making, boating, shooting and old home restoration and rehabilitation. He used to hunt large and small game and birds, but he hasn't done that in the past few years. Dick became a volunteer at Patriots Point in September 2012.

Volunteering in the Vietnam Experience at Patriot's Point gives me the opportunity to meet many, many new and delightful visitors, who are interested in learning about service in Viet Nam. Occasionally, a Vietnamese ex-patriot family would come in who often had been living in the same area in which I serviced. The best part of my time there is meeting other Vietnam veterans and exchanging war stories and a few laughs. Hard to believe that it was such a long time ago and was such a formative experience for the rest of my life. I have many fond memories of my military service. I wouldn't have missed it for anything.

CHAPTER 6

VOLUNTEER, "SCOTTY" ANDREWS

★★★

Scotty Andrews: Photo property of author

I asked "Scotty" to provide some stories for possible publishing in *Short Rations From Patriots Point Volunteers,* prompting this initial reply from him:

I might have a story for you; however, as you are a Marine, I'm not sure how you will take it. So, I decided to submit it anyway. Basically, here is the crux:

I joined the Navy as otherwise I would have been drafted and thought the opportunity to travel, and see the world, would be more possible as a sailor. Which it was, with all those visits to European, and other ports from Athens to Valencia included. Even Beirut which was possible at that time, I enjoyed visiting. Also remember, France was a member of NATO at that time, and we were home ported in Ville France on the French Rivera. All those opportunities to meet such interesting people. Rota redux: I also thought the uniforms were cool. What young lady could resist a young man in dress whites? This served me in good stead, not only for the leadership opportunities but, later on, for a career in international banking and finance with a number of organizations such as Citicorp, a number of other banks, the World Bank, Coopers and Lybrand Consulting which took me all over the world from Europe, to Latin America. Also to the Far, Middle, and Near East, Africa, etc. I also had a position as Managing Director of Major Projects at the Overseas Investment Corporation (OPIC) under the Reagan Administration where I not only held a Diplomatic Passport, but also my second Top Secret clearance. The first when I was on the Admiral's Staff in Panama/ Canal Zone. I Also lived overseas for about ten years from London to Warsaw. My brief but fulfilling naval career also afforded me the GI Bill benefits which helped finance my MBA degree. I am proud to be Navy, through and through.

But, now let's get into the meat of my Navy days.

After I finished Navy Officers Candidate School (OCS) in November of 1964, I was assigned to the carrier the USS *Forrestal*, yes that same one that later suffered a disaster in the Pacific. Let me just quote from internet historical sources, to relay what happened: *On 29 July 1967, a fire broke out on board the aircraft carrier USS Forrestal. An electrical problem had caused the discharge of a Zuni rocket on the flight deck, triggering a chain-reaction of explosions that killed 134 sailors and injured 161. At the time, Forrestal was engaged in combat operations in the Gulf of Tonkin, during the Vietnam War. The ship survived with damage exceeding 72 million dollars, not including the cost of damaged aircraft.* Thankfully, I had two deployments with the 6th Fleet in the Mediterranean Sea (MED), and then had another assignment or two. And, so we begin.

Normally, in those days, young, and yes even some older recruits were given a choice—either jail or the military service. It was quiet common. A lot of young men came into the military and naval service through that route. So, bear this in mind as we proceed with the story. Upon reporting to the USS *Forrestal* after OCS in November of 1964, I was told I would be responsible for the 4th Division, the Boatswains Mates. Please understand the Navy 4th Division takes less technical skills being primarily responsible for the more traditional shipboard duties, such as controlling liberty boats, captains gig, and in our case, the admiral's barge, also refueling and replenishing at sea, chipping paint, swabbing decks, etc. Normally these sailors carry knives to help with their jobs. Considering many of these young men came into the Navy through the civilian criminal court system . . . Well! Enough said. You get the picture. Anyway, upon being advised that one of my responsibilities included being assigned as First Rifle Platoon Commander, and as such was also in charge of the landing party. This platoon was composed of some of my 4th Division sailors as well as some of the Marines who were attached to the Marine Air Squadron we had on board. Now you have to remember, we young navy officers had absolutely zero fire arms training at OCS. Part of my assignment was to take my platoon into a small boat and circle the ship while at anchor, when in potentially dangerous and/or Communist countries, which, in this case included Italy which had a Communist government at the time.

OK, so how was my shipboard weapons training addressed? No lie, you gotta believe this, the Marines took me to the fantail of the carrier, and gave me instruction in the use of; get this, the famous THOMPSON SUB MACHINE GUN. Picture me spraying the vast Mediterranean Sea with .45 cal. slugs from a bucking sub-machine gun with projectiles splashing into the sea from Gibraltar to Cyprus. My Navy platoon members were provided with Garand M-1s, of WWII and Korean War vintage. WWII all over again. Then, on a daily basis, I went off to circle the ship, normally in the evening, for example the 12 Midnight to 4 am watch, called the mid-watch. FYI, as green as I was, I gathered up all of my crew's weapons and put them securely under my seat as if I was concerned that they might be inclined to shoot someone, or, more importantly—shoot me. Not a good way to end this wonderful in-port duty.

Now, one might ask why they didn't assign an onboard Marine officer for this duty. Well, my only guess was that they considered the liberty boat we used as a ship? And, what Navy officer wants a Marine in charge of a ship? Anyhow, that's my theory.

Wait! Let's back up a bit. I know, I'm jumping around, Hang with me. Enroute to *Forrestal,* the story gets even goofier. I flew into Rota Spain from New Jersey. As I got on the aircraft in Jersey, someone gave me a briefcase supposedly filled with top secret or secret papers, handcuffed me to the case, and away I go to Rota. Me, and another ensign as passengers. Oh yeah! I also had wrapped around my waist a .45 pistol, which of course I had never fired before. Further, I was told someone at Rota would take the case, handcuffs, and pistol from me. Thankfully! Upon landing, and being relieved of my *Top Secret* burden, I felt better that my *secret* mission was over. At Rota, we were to be picked up by one of the *Forrestal* aircraft. Me, and this other young Ensign were supposed to board this aircraft heading for *Forrestal.* Then, I found out that my personal gear, uniforms, etc., with one exception, was sent not to Spain, but elsewhere. They didn't know exactly where but promised it would be found. They didn't say WHEN it would be found.

That exception was my Navy Officers' sword which I personally carried on board the aircraft and aboard the *Forrestal.* In retrospect, I guess it (the sword) could have been helpful if we actually had to use my landing party to rescue some poor Americans harassed at some Italian Restaurant, or seedy flamingo joint, for example. Even today, I could picture myself leading a landing party as Marine Captain Jerome, in the1975 movie *The Wind and the Lion*, disposing some sultan from his throne with the point of my officer's sword. These bouts of fantasy have faded with time. Thankfully!

Nowadays, a retired Marine colonel, the guy I play tennis with, did not believe my story about my platoon leadership abilities as a naval officer, which I must admit were zero, I actually showed him a copy of my orders confirming this bold plan to get me, my sword, and top secret documents aboard the aircraft carrier. Upon reviewing the old yellowing orders, he left shaking his head. Stoney, I will text you a copy thereof.

If you decide to use this little missive above, here is something you probably won't use: I digress again. Bear with me. While in Rota waiting for the aircraft going to *Forrestal,* I borrowed a sport coat from a guy named Dennis. Remember my Navy clothing was MIA. Off I go to town in my Navy clothing covered by a sport coat. I end up in some flamingo joint. Alas, in true Navy fashion I met a fair lady and spent the evening with her. Upon returning to the BOQ in the morning, I found out that I had missed the plane sent from the *Forrestal.* The other ensign had made the flight and I was a "no show." I was very concerned about what they might do to me, and although I was tempted to visit a flamingo joint again, I stayed in the boring BOQ. To my surprise no one seemed to mind when the next flight came out to pick me up. I guess expectations of a shiny, new ninety-day-wonder Naval Reserve Officer was pretty low on the bar. In any case, I landed on the *Forrestal* on a Willie Fudd (a Grumman WF (E-1) Tracer, twin engine, propeller-driven aircraft) soon afterward off the coast of Naples, my one and only carrier landing. That's quite an introduction to Navy life in the 1960s.

I only had one other assignment after the two Med deployments (we had a very quick turnaround as the USS *America* had hit a ship and was out of commission, and we needed two carriers active in the Med at that time), and that was on an admiral's staff in the then US Canal Zone

(Commander US Naval Forces Southern Command, Fourth Naval District) A little more on that a little bit later.

In any event, when we went back to Norfolk for a quick refit, I was sent to the Anti-Sub, and CIC (Combat Information Center) Watch Officers School. As you guessed, during my second deployment I served as a CIC Watch Officer in addition to my normal watches on the bridge. That was working with a much different kind of sailor (my landing party gig was only from time to time and that terminated after my CIC assignment). FYI, I also stood bridge watches when I was with the 4th Division in addition to serving as a gunnery officer and going after pilots when they went in the drink (only once did I go after a downed pilot in the drink, but a helo got the pilot before us); however, being put into the sea during a storm was very exciting indeed on at least two counts, maybe three, getting off the carrier and back on again while the swells bashed against the ship, as well as riding up and down the swells when looking for the pilot, was an adventure. Also one of my guys had a rifle in the event of sharks and the other was steering the boat. A couple of things here, you will note I was not entrusted with the rifle, and as crew are thought to be more valuable than new ensigns, it appears in addition to commanding yet another boat in extremis, I apparently was to go into the sea to assist the pilot if necessary. Thank God for the helos success. To finish my sea experience story, I guess after my initial mishaps, I turned out to be not a bad sailor, in fact received a commendation from RADM O' Brien, then Commander Cruiser, Destroyer Flotilla Ten embarked for services performed in CIC as Watch Officer when we were "playing" with a Russian sub. He came down to CIC for a part of the 12-4 mid-watch. I was more than surprised as it seemed quite normal to me. There were plenty of Russian ships at that time.

As to the Canal Zone and Panama. A couple of perhaps interesting things: hunting cougars in the jungle with every kind of snake you can think of, but maybe I'll leave that for another later tale. However, just one quick note. RADM Johnson, insisted that the Navy (many of us),

Marine (two of them), and Coast Guard (two also) officers challenge the Army and Air Force officers to a game of flag football. Believe it when I say, it was televised from coast to coast in the fifty-mile-width of the Canal Zone. Well, we being basically a bunch of staff officers had quite a time taking on primarily Special Forces Army officers undergoing pretty rugged training for deployment to Vietnam, which was then heating up in those days. To be brief, I could not literally get out of bed for two days afterwards. The young ladies at our "victory" party were very understanding. I couldn't move! And, as of this missive, I am still waiting for my "purple heart."

Sorry, I jumped around a little bit. It's in my nature. Let me know if you need any clarification.

What do you enjoy about volunteering here?

I enjoy my volunteer duty on the Yorktown as it permits me to meet guests from all over the world, in addition to former military types where we can beguile one another with our tales of days of yore.

Hope this helps. If you have any questions you can always reach me on my cell. I truly enjoy your editing which makes my experiences even more interesting. Best,

Then, here is another Scotty Andrews addition:

If my earlier stories sound improbable, this one is truly unbelievable. But, it really happened: While we were in Palma de Majorca awaiting our relief by another carrier in the 6th fleet, as we had finished our deployment, can't actually remember if it was my first or second; anyhow, I met a British model, Pat Wellington, who was doing a shoot for Marlboro cigarettes there. Well, she invited me to join her in London, if I could get leave to do so. My boss said OK. So, I prepare to leave for London when, the evening before I was to leave, I met a gorgeous blond girl from Sweden. Major choice here—bird in the hand or English model in London? Using all my courage I opted for the unknown and stayed with London. It was actually a mews apartment in Hampstead Heath, an apartment above a stable, quite fashionable at that time. I wondered about my choice, as we hit a terrific electrical storm on the flight to London, which I imagined the Swedish girl had sent as repayment for my ultimate choice. By the way, this same girl introduced me to Scotch and milk which had some merit which I cannot remember—aphrodisiac?

Anyway here is when it gets really unreal. Pat picked me up in her Triumph sports car and off we went, OK so far nothing special. On the way we stopped at a friend's apartment in London where a party was going on. Another famous model at the time, Jean Shrimpton, was there; now hold on, and Julie Christie and Pete O'Toole. Too much I know; Julie had just finished the movie, "Darling" which made her name, later more famously in "Dr. Zhivago." Ok, deep breath: As we continue. Pat excused that she would temporarily put me up in a nearby hotel as a friend was also staying with her at the time. After staying in the hotel for a short time, I'm thinking screw this. I came all this way for nothing. In any event, she collected me and off to her place we go. In any case, the bed was still warm, but alas the Navy had triumphed in dispatching an interloper, who-ever-he-was. It was so revealing, seeing her before and after her morning bath and made-up face, as she was doing a number of commercials at that time. Her face was plastered all over London, on numerous billboards, in the tube, and elsewhere. Well I did my best to represent the Navy, like I always did.

Subsequently, I joined her in a shoot in Zurich, where we checked in and out of a hotel in the same day, before her departure back to London and my departure back to Frankfort. I took the train to Frankfort to get a military hop back to good ole USA. The plane stopped in Chateauroux air base in France, which was still a member of NATO at that time. The flight was scheduled for the next evening. During the evening layover, I made a telephone call to London to bid farewell to Pat. I was staying at the BOQ and the call was made through a base operator who was French. After the call to Pat, we, the telephone operator and me, continued to talk. Yes, you've guessed it, a wonderful evening with my new friend, and once again no need to use the BOQ to sleep alone. Vive le France!

It was a boring bit from Frankfurt, on an old prop job which seemed to be going backward at times, first to Keflavik, Iceland for an evening, and then back to the US and reality. Oh, at Frankfurt, I joined some Army paratroopers returning to the US and the plane was rigged up for them to actually make jumps. We played poker and I got lucky and was advised I might make my first jump, sans parachute. Sore losers, these Army guys.

Scotty Andrews (the swordsman) Lt. jg USNR

CHAPTER 7

DAVID MILLMAN, PATRIOTS POINT VOLUNTEER

★★★

Photo property of author. David is aboard the USS Monitor. Inside the turret at Mariners Museum, Newport News, VA. Working on 2 Dahlgren cannons, in 2004.

Here is a small background of David Millman. It's all I knew about the man until we each agreed to meet for a beer after volunteer work one day:

David was born in New York City and raised on Long Island. He attended W.C. Mepham High School. He then graduated from Lassen

College in Susanville, California, with a degree in Gunsmithing. David was a Chief Gunners Mate in the US Coast Guard from 1984 to 2004. He served on the Coastguard Cutters, *Sitiknak, Sherman* and *Dallas.* He also served two years as an instructor at Yorktown, Virginia. He is trained on all small arms and shipboard weapon systems found on *Yorktown* and *Laffey*. David became a Patriots Point volunteer in September 2016.

That's it. That's all I knew until those beers. Now, let's let David do some talking:

"I'm David Millman, a volunteer at the Naval and Maritime Museum at Patriots Point. I've been asked by Ralph Stoney Bates, another volunteer, and an author of several published books, to tell a bit about myself for potential publication in a book to be titled *Short Rations From Patriots Point Volunteers.* At first, I couldn't think of anything I have done in my life worthy of publishing. Then, I met Stoney at a bar, and by the fourth or fifth beer I had related half a dozen "sea-stories" with clarity and truthfulness contained therein. Wow! I've had quite a life. Let me share some of those stories with you:

RAT GUARD (1990)

"I was stationed on the USCGC *SITKINAK* WPB-1329 in Key West, FL and had duty as Officer of the Day (OOD) when I got a call from the Group Command Center. They told me a small boat was towing in a Cuban barge that had been adrift in the Florida Straits and had removed it as a hazard to navigation. What does this have to do with me? I'm thinking! Then the punchline. Group wants me to report to the seizure pier (where we tied up and searched vessels for illegal drugs or migrants) with an M-16. I told them I could not leave the ship. They told me they had already spoken to my Commanding Officer (CO), that I should wake up my duty engineer, and they would send someone over (who was not rifle qualified) to help stand the watch. I called my CO at home and he said to do what Group wants. So I grabbed an ammo belt and a rifle and walked over to the seizure pier thinking I would be guarding some Cuban migrants 'til immigration showed up. But that didn't make sense since normally we would guard prisoners with a Law Enforcement belt and a handgun. When I got there the Group OOD was watching the station crew tie up the barge.

He said to me, "Stand here 'till a decision is made on what to do with this barge and shoot anything that tries to get on shore."

I replied, "You mean people?" more than a little shocked. That certainly wasn't our Use of Force policy.

His response was, "No. I mean rats, dogs, cats, even mice. Here's a radio in case you actually shoot anything so people don't panic if they hear gun fire."

So, for the next two hours I stood my watch as a human rat guard against that animal invasion of Station Key West. Nothing dared to make the attempt. Finally, I was relieved when the station took it back in tow and took it off shore to scuttle it.

I then went back to my ship to make the most bizarre log entry I ever made or had ever seen, other than a 0000-0400 entry on New Year's Eve! More on that entry later.

Here are two more from my trips to the Med and Black Sea:

METRIC (1999)

"On a patrol to the Med on the USCGC *Dallas* (WHEC 716), we pulled into Antalya, Turkey to do some training with the Turkish Coast Guard (CG). We docked at the cruise ship pier, as the Coast Guard station's pier on the other side of town was way too small. The OPS boss, WEPO, and I were driven over to the CG station for a presentation on the Turkish CGs assets and capabilities. During the show a slide of various cutters came up and a very proud Turkish LT told me he was the captain of one of the largest cutters in the fleet. He said, "That is my ship. It is thirty meters long."

"After the briefing, we were driving back to the *Dallas* and the same LT (lieutenant) asked me how long our cutter was. I told him 125 meters. He did his conversion and shook his head. "No, you must be wrong. There are no cutters that big. You Americans never use metric properly."

I replied, "I work on an Italian gun system and use metric every day."

"He still said I was mistaken. We pulled on to the pier and parked by the brow. We all got out and there was the LT, speechless, mouth open, staring in amazement at the *Dallas*.

Smiling, I walked up to him and stated, "I told you I know how to use metric."

Note: Dallas was 378 ft. long.

STAMPEDE (1999)

"On patrol in the Black Sea, USCGC Dallas (WHEC 716), we pulled into Poti, Republic of Georgia. One of the events was a memorial wreath ceremony for the soldiers of The Great Patriotic War (WWII, in the west) at a statue outside of town. The Russians drove up in a bus and picked up the ten Coasties who had volunteered, which included me. We drove about five miles to a clearing in the forest which had a large memorial of Russian Soldiers liberating the Motherland. We got out and formed an Honor Guard to escort the Wreath to the base of the memorial. We then started to hear movement in the woods to our right. It got disturbingly louder. A bull broke thru the tree line followed by a few cows, all running like their lives depended on it. We looked at the Russians, who were standing frozen. Quickly, one of them, who spoke some English, yelled for everyone to get inside the bus. We all made it as about 100 more cattle tore through the clearing, shaking the bus violently and disappeared into the woods on the left. When the dust cleared, one of the Russians grabbed an AK-47 and went outside and slowly patrolled around the clearing. He finally gave what must have been an all clear, as the Russian who spoke English said "Let's try again." Amazingly the wreath had survived and we were able to complete the ceremony. If we hadn't had the bus to hide in, there might be a memorial to the ten Coastics killed in a stampede in far off Russia.

Here is another:

EIGHTY ROUNDS A MINUTE (MAY 1991)

I was stationed on the USCGC *SITKINAK* WPB-1329 in Key West, FL and we were tasked with showing the flag and doing tours for Armed Forces Day at Mallory Square. We dressed ship and put on dress uniforms and sailed around the bight to the pier at Mallory Square with the USS HERCULES PHM-2, a Pegasus class hydrofoil. After many tours, I got a break and never having been inside a hydrofoil, I joined the next tour group. A LTJG gave the tour and gave a good description of the MK 75/76mm 62 cal. gun mount. When he was done and moved to the next point for his tour, an elderly man, maybe in his 90s, got my attention (I guess because I was in uniform).

He asked, "Did he say this gun fires eighty rounds a minute?"

I replied "Yes, this gun can fire up to eighty rounds a minute."

He was quiet for a while and repeated "Eighty?"

"Yes, eighty."

"A minute?"

"Yes, eighty rounds a minute."

Silence.

Then he said "Back in WWI, if we fired our French 75mm guns more than six rounds an hour, we would get yelled at for wearing out the barrels!" That guy was a WW1 artillery man.

Now I really took a closer look at this old-time veteran, and proceeded in giving him a very detailed description of the gun mount, it's cooling system, and how it could fire that fast. Made my day!

AN UNUSUAL LOOKOUT REPORT TO THE BRIDGE (APRIL 1990)

"I told you I'd get to this—I was on patrol on the USCGC SITKINAK WPB-1329, standing lookout on the 0000-0400 watch off the east coast of Florida on a course of 090. Around 0200 the gauge glass on the console began to glow with an orange light. Soon the entire ship was lit up by a bright orange blaze of light like a fire. I turned around and finally had the presence of mind to make the following report:

"Bridge, I have a sky contact aft bearing 180, Space Shuttle Discovery, position angle 20... No 30, er, 40, no, 50, now 60, it's gone!!!"

My best sighting report ever.

COAST ARTILLERY (JUNE 1998)

"I was stationed at the Pacific Area Law Enforcement Training Team, and we had provided training for the National Park Service Rangers. To thank us, they offered some tours to sites in Northern California. I took a tour of the Coast Artillery Forts in the Marin Headlands Park north of the Golden Gate. During the tour, the Ranger was describing the function of all the structures of the fort until we came to a concrete platform about 8 by 4 foot with 2 foot walls around it on three sides. The ranger said "We do not know what this was used for. We have researched original blue prints and photos and can find no reference to this structure." One of the other persons in the tour raised his hand. The ranger said "Yes sir." The man said, "My dad was in the Coast Artillery. I use to visit him here. That's where we keep the garbage cans."

"Listen, there's a few other interesting events occurring during my active duty with the US Coast Guard. Often they come to me in interesting ways. Someone will say a word or utter a phrase, and, "Bingo!" it hits me. Here's an example:

SHANGHAI'D (1995)

"On patrol on the USCGC *Sherman* (WHEC-720) in the Pacific enforcing a ban on high seas drift netting (nets that can be up to forty miles long and kill everything that gets caught, not just the targeted fish), we detained a Chinese fishing vessel illegally using drift nets. They said they were Taiwanese, but when the state department sorted it out, they were Red Chinese and we were directed to take them to Shanghai and turn them over to the Chinese military. The Sherman became the first US Coast Guard cutter to ever enter Red Chinese waters. We were not allowed to tie up to a pier and were directed to anchor out in the harbor.

"That afternoon a patrol boat about sixty feet long approached with the highest ranking Chinese military person they could find, an army general in his dress uniform with all his decorations on display. Our boarding party, led by an ensign (ENS), began to make the transfer of the fishing boat and its contents to the general on his boat, but the general couldn't take his eyes off the *Sherman*. With a MK 75 gun, Harpoon missiles, torpedo tubes, and a CIWS, you could read the thought on his face.

If that's the US Coast Guard, what does the US Navy look like?, was written all over it.

"I have more stories or is this enough material from me?" David asked.

"Send 'em as you feel 'em, David," was my response. It caused a flood:

Here's another:

RED SCARE (1984)

"I was in my third week of boot camp at Cape May, NJ doing something menial in the squad bay, when the dreaded Assistant Company Commander (ACC) entered, and worse said, "Millman, report to the Company Commander's office." This was never for something other than a disaster. I ran out to the hall way and stood out of sight in the hall by the office door.

"Recruit Millman reporting as ordered," I yelled out.

Then the dreaded "Square It," came in a growling response.

I entered and stood at attention.

"Millman, we got a disturbing piece of mail for you." The ACC handed me a post card. It was from my parents back in Long Island, NY.

"Are you a member of the communist party?"

"I looked at the picture on the front of the card. It was the living room of Sagamore Hill. Above the main seats hangs a red flag with a blue star in the middle with many small white stars around it.

"This is Sagamore Hill," I said.

Blank stares were directed at the suspected commie.

"Theodore Roosevelt's house."

More blank stares.

"Speak softly, big stick," I added hopefully.

"The flag was a gift from Texas, the Lone Star State, and the little stars are cities in the state," I almost pleaded.

Dead silence for about two minutes.

The ACC took the post card back and said, "Go back to the squad bay." I retreated as fast as possible.

Thirty minutes later, we had mail call. I then received, my now not so disturbing, post card with no comment whatsoever.

My being suspected as being a Communist Party member had passed. Thankfully!

After a brief hiatus, and as David was traveling, this event was sent to me:

SHARK RIVER (1985)

"While stationed at Station Shark River, NJ, my 41 ft. boat crew was underway off the coast conducting training with a HH3F Sea Guard helicopter from Air Station Brooklyn. We were practicing hoists of people and rescue equipment, when we received a radio call from the USCGC *Cape Starr* (WPB-95320), asking us to stop a vessel they were chasing north along the coast. It was a white cabin cruiser with no numbering or name visible (all US vessels must have a name and homeport or state numbers). We all looked south and could see the vessel and the much slower cutter in pursuit. Then the pilot of the helo said "I got this." He flew straight at the vessel and began a hover about thirty feet in front of the bridge, and slowly flew backwards until the vessel stopped. That was the most aggressive flying I would ever see. This was better than any TV show! We then boarded the vessel while our watchdog hovered above. The captain stated he was a boat dealer and was taking the vessel to a boat show in New York City. He pleaded ignorance that he needed numbers for a demo boat (not believed) and that he didn't notice the 95 ft. cutter behind him (also not believed). Even so, this was a fineable offense, and since those were the only issues, the boarding officer citied him for a violation on the 4100 boarding report. We finished the boarding and resumed training with the helo and the *Cape Starr.*

"Later that afternoon the boarding officer filled out a SEER (summary of enforcement events report) which was actually done in pencil, then formatted and sent by message on a really slow computer. Two days later, two FBI agents came to the station and wanted to talk to everyone involved in the boarding. They showed us a picture of various men and asked if any of them were on the boat we had boarded. One of the other crewmen identified one of the people that was hanging back in the cabin. 'What's the interest,' he asked. 'He's wanted for first degree murder,' one of the agents responded.

Better than TV!"

NAUTICAL TITLES:

"In my underway travels with the Coast Guard, I have earned a number of Nautical titles by crossing various places on the ocean:

GOLDEN SHELLBACK. The combination of GOLDEN DRAGON (crossing the International dateline) and SHELLBACK (crossing the equator).

ORDER of the DITCH (transit the Panama Canal).

ORDER of the SPANISH MAIN (transit the Caribbean Sea).

ORDER of the PILLARS of HERCULES (transit the Strait of Gibraltar).

The REALM of the CZAR (transit the Dardanelles and the Bosporus from the Mediterranean to the Black Sea).

PLANKOWNER of USCGC SITKINAK WPB -1329 (original crew-members of a newly commissioned warship)."

I will do more bio next time.

Editor's Note: Gotta finish the story of the BEER'S: David and I agreed to meet after volunteer duty one day, and the Kickin Chicken Bar and Grill, on Coleman Boulevard in Mt.

Pleasant, was selected. We met at the bar. I bought a round, David bought a round, I bought another, ditto, David. We were all set to leave with me having a couple of stories in my notes, when the bartender bought a round. After a couple of more stories were flowing from David, we started to leave, again, when a customer on the other side of the bar, exercising patriotic duty, bought a round for us. Later, now armed with half a dozen stories about David and the USCG, I made some excuse about some pending disaster, and departed the Kickin Chicken. David remained at the bar. It seems that our Patriots Point Volunteer uniform, his Coast Guard cover, and my Marine Corps cover combined with our loud story-telling, created a sense of unique patriotism in the onlookers, resulting in a couple of free beers and additional stories.

CHAPTER 8

VOLUNTEER BRUCE "WOODY" CAINE

★★★

Woody Caine: Photo property of author

"Woody" grew up expecting to be a soldier. He realized his dream by earning a Regular Army Commission in the Infantry in 1966, and spent twenty-six years in a wide range of challenging Army assignments. He seems incapable of really retiring. When he isn't teaching or greeting visitors to *The Vietnam Experience*, he is researching and building military model dioramas of historical relevance.

Bruce "Woody" Caine grew up on Long Island. He received a B.S. in Biology from the College of William & Mary in 1966, an MBA in social psychology from the University of Florida in 1975, and a PhD in social psychology from the University of Florida in 1976. He served in the Army from 1966 to 1992, with a specialty in armored cavalry. He served in Germany from 1966 to 1968 and 1968 to 1972. He served in Vietnam from 1968 to 1969, where he served in Vietnam's Mekong Delta as an adviser with the (Republic of Vietnam) RVN Army. From 1976 to 1979, he taught at West Point. He was head of the Department of Military Science at Northeast Missouri State University from 1982 to 1985 and director of the Army Officer Education (ROTC) at Vanderbilt University from 1988 to 1992. Bruce taught psychology at Vanderbilt University for over thirty-five years, retiring in 2014. He is a professor of the practice of human & organization development. Bruce became a Patriots Point volunteer in January 2015.

SOME "WOODY" STORIES

One of the best things about volunteering at *The Vietnam Experience* at Patriots Point Naval and Maritime Museum is meeting and listening to the stories of veterans and family members who are inspired by our displays and sounds. These tangible images tend to reflect intangible shared experiences voiced by many of our visitors, not shared with any-one before.

My favorite, of these of shared experiences, are the product of certain visitors' examination of our Naval Support Base buildings, each of which was built to be as historically accurate as possible. Former combat engineers, including Navy Sea Bees, of the Vietnam era have verified this, but some have added comments that must be shared:

One Army Engineer asked me if I knew what teams like his used to construct these versatile and durable buildings. Before I could answer, he said "We used leftover packing materials. Lots of things like that helicopter (pointing to a UH -1M) came to 'Nam in crates. All that plywood and 2 by 4s never went to waste. We used lots of packing pallets for walkways. Great for keeping your feet dry."

Another engineer veteran who served with artillery units asked me why we hadn't insulated our building's roofs with Styrofoam. I said "Where would units in Vietnam have gotten enough to do that?" His reply, "Shipping material around artillery rounds."

And then, there was the very proud combat engineer who, having inspected all of our buildings came up to me and said "Yup. You got 'em right. Even the latrine." And then he added, "I ought to know. Built a dozen of those while I was in 'Nam." You just have to admire pride of ownership.

But it was an "old grunt" a former generator mechanic, who, while acknowledging how critical his job was to maintaining the operation of any base, claimed he regularly volunteered to clean out the half-cut 55 gallon drums used to collect human waste in the back of latrines and burn it, because "When I finished the burn, no one would mess with me for a week." It was simply an elegant process for avoiding additional duties, and harassment by overly demanding superiors.

Those half drums, filled with human waste, were burned by dragging the container(s) from the head or latrine, applying gasoline or diesel fuel to the contents, setting it ablaze, and absorbing the aroma of the fumes through clothing, hair, and every single body pore. The aroma lasted for days. You get the picture. This was just part of the practice of sound field sanitation by soldiers in the field.

Another story which I love to share with visitors involves a group of ladies who served in Vietnam with the USO (United Services Organization). Nicknamed "donut dollies" by GIs, these once young ladies related tales of visits to fire bases and hospitals that I wish I had recorded. But there was one lady who stood transfixed on our dock next to our green PBR (Patrol Boat River), transfixed just looking and staring at it. I asked "Are you OK?" to which she replied, "Oh yes. That's my boat." When I started to reply, she explained, "Oh I know it's not really mine but you see when I was in Vietnam, I met and fell in love with a boat captain and he named his boat after me. My name is Elaine, and when that young stud came home, I married him and I still got him parked at home now."

I have no idea where the name Elaine that graces our PBR came from, but to me this story is as good an explanation as any could be.

As a volunteer, one of my hobbies is building military miniatures. I've been doing it for many years as a way of training myself to pay attention to detail and to slow down my hyperactivity. So when Patriots Point decided to erect a Quonset hut to serve as a display area for The Vietnam Experience, I offered to build a set of dioramas – terrain scenes mounting boats used by the Brown Water Navy, tanks, armored personnel carriers, trucks and other vehicles used by the Army and Marine Corps in Vietnam. These models attract attention as they were intended to but also provoke some vivid memories.

One former mechanized infantryman who served two tours in 'Nam proudly told his grandkids how he had maneuvered his APC (M-113 Armored Personnel Carrier) through dense jungle and rubber trees claiming "It was harder than driving in California traffic on the freeway." He went on to describe how he armored his driver's compartment with every extra flak vest he could find.

During his second tour, he was an infantry squad leader and rode to battle in the armored vehicle commander's hatch with its .50 caliber

M2 heavy barrel machinegun. Two of the models in the display case show this "ACAV" modification to the M-113. One grandson remarked "Boy, I'll bet it was hot. Did you ever burn your hand on the gun shield, Grandad?" The "old soldier" just smiled, glanced at his hands, and said "Well, maybe."

One of the dioramas displays a light armored vehicle used by the Marines called an "ONTOS." A number of veterans have shaken their heads, reflecting memories, none of which seem favorable, of this under-powered, overly armed device. As done by the Marines, with my model, I dismounted one of the six 106mm recoilless rifles from this vehicle and placed it on a fondly remembered mechanical mule. This cargo carrier served nobly as a weapons carrier, able to climb hills (if slowly) and move down narrow passages between buildings in cities like Hue where we relearned the art of combat in cities. It was also sometimes used to get wounded personnel to safety. The driver could actually crawl on the ground while driving the mule. The veterans enjoy showing their families the actual "mechanical mule" we have on display at *The Vietnam Experience.*

The sister of a Navy SEAL who served in Vietnam enjoyed seeing the UDT (Underwater Demolition Team) boat in the display. She remarked that her brother told of checking the hulls of cargo ships in the harbor for enemy emplaced mines, and the risky task of removing them. She smiled when she said he preferred this duty to being a scout sitting waist-deep in a rice paddy watching for enemy movement, another task assigned to the SEALS, because he was impatient and really hated being wet and dirty, so solitary in the water of a rice paddy on observation duty wasn't for him.

This listening and encouragement sharing, often allows me as a storyteller, to respond with a few bits of insight of my own. I am often asked about my experiences in Vietnam, to which I reply "It was a tremendous learning experience for a young, inexperienced combat arms officer, because I had the good fortune to be assigned to serve as the Combat Assistance Team Leader (formerly called Advisor) to a Vietnamese Infantry Battalion, commanded by one of the most honorable, ethical, compassionate and skillful leaders I have ever met." This comment often leads to requests for examples of what I learned.

Each of the following illustrates a lesson that I have shared in my leadership development classes and workshops over many years:

Dai Uy (Captain) My had been fighting his nation's enemies for ten years when I joined his unit in the center of the Mekong Delta, and I quickly discovered that his unit was highly disciplined, physically fit, and willing to fight. Many of the soldiers in this unit had been recruited by Dai Uy My from within his area of operations (AO). Their family connections and familiarity with the terrain were sources of support for the battalion and intelligence on "strangers in the area" who most often were North Vietnamese soldiers infiltrated into our AO from Cambodia, or local "gangsters" marginally aligned with the few operational Viet Cong units remaining in the area by early 1969.

<u>The leadership lesson here is</u>: Build a deep and wide understanding of your "area of operations," develop reliable sources of information, seek alliances, and treat others fairly and honestly.

The unit also had draftees assigned from other areas of the country and Dai Uy My had assigned each of these young men to a local, telling the pair, "Each of you knows things the other does not. So teach each other." To the local soldier, he would say "Show this brother how to live well in the Delta like you do." And to the city soldier, he would say "Explain to your brother how things work in the city or in your village." And, to the two, "Your task is to take care of each other."

<u>The leadership lesson here is:</u> build teamwork, cohesion, mutual support and honest caring starting with the buddy pair and grow it from there.

Dai Uy My lived consistently by three leadership rules that I have adopted as my own. They are:

Never waste a soldier's life. (By which he meant don't waste their time, their energy, their creativity, their dedication.)

Never fight a fight you can't win. (By which he meant set the odds in your favor or back off until you can control the situation and the outcome.)

See the thing that shouldn't be there. (Which was his way of teaching his soldiers to spot booby traps and other threats, but he also meant see the things that needed fixing – opportunities and innovation, shortcoming, and preventative maintenance actions to avoid failures and to keep things running.)

One particular day a Swedish gentleman, who works for VOLVO, visited *The Vietnamese Experience* and heard me recite these examples. He asked me to repeat the three rules and to explain them more fully, which I did. He visited again a few weeks later and asked me to write down the rules which he sincerely felt he could apply to his own management actions. I gladly did so and we discussed how these "combat" ideas apply to civil business. Just recently, he returned again, this time with his son. We reviewed again how these five lessons have been validated over and over by effective teams and organizations.

Yes, I was very lucky to be assigned to this battalion and to have Dai Uy My as my mentor at a critical point of my development as a soldier and a leader.

I do get asked what I actually did as a Combat Assistance Team Leader, and I'm happy to point out that I rarely gave tactical advice (given my lack of combat experience early on) but that I did provided active liaison contacts with American units, most often Navy, Army and Coast Guard

Riverine units (Brown Water Navy), as well as Navy and Air Force strike aircraft to insure effective coordination and to avoid incidents.

But, I quickly discovered I had some well-developed talents in operational functions the unit sorely needed. The first of these was emergency medical care, field sanitation and preventative medicine. The unit's medics needed additional training and I was able to provide it, with the support of the American Medevac crews that worked our area. I ended up carrying a large medical bag with everything from minor surgery kits to ointments to treat skin infections, and using all of them. One of my most valuable "magic cures" was brown lye-based laundry soap that remarkably served as a deterrent to leeches. Not exactly an Infantryman's load, but helpful in many situations.

The Mekong Delta has 5000 miles of rivers and canals, and my Vietnamese infantry unit on operational sweeps typically crossed up to a dozen of these waterways of various widths and depths daily. I realized that in the rainy season many of these crossing could not be made "on-foot" as they simply were not fordable. If boats or sampans could not be found, the troops needed to swim the canal or stream. But many of the city or mountain-raised soldiers had never learned to swim, unlike most of the Delta "kids" who could.

So, as a former ocean beach lifeguard, swim instructor and waterfront director for the Boy Scouts, it quickly fell to me to swim across each canal trailing two or more ropes to tie off on the other side, so once the troops had packed their gear in poncho rafts, they could pull themselves across using the ropes. As an extra safety measure, I would position myself downstream with one or two Vietnamese swimmers I coached on techniques, to act as a rescue team.

In the evenings when we set up a night defensive position along a canal, I taught swimming to those soldiers who wished to learn. On other evenings, I taught English to a group of young men who wanted to become pilots. Again, not exactly what my job description prescribed, but through these interactions, I learned so much about their ancient culture and the strengths of these soldiers who accepted me into their ranks. I show visitors a few pictures in my scrapbook to illustrate these somewhat unique experiences.

When prompted by a visitor, I will tell the story of my homecoming from Vietnam. This request is usually a result of seeing one or two of the stories in our Vietnam Experiences video. One of the commentators describes how soldiers returning were told at the US airport to take off their uniforms and not to discuss their tour with anyone. Another related the pain he and his buddies felt when they were called "baby killers" by protesters.

In response, I tell the following tale. I was approaching the end of my one year tour and had received both orders for reassignment to Germany and the ticket for my scheduled flight home. My Vietnamese unit was on a short break at home base in Sa Dec City, and I welcomed my replacement, anticipating about two weeks of overlap. But things do happen. The unit went out for a one day sweep basically to "show the flag." It was rainy season and everyone got wet, then dry, wet again, and dry again, throughout the operation. When I went to find my replacement the next morning, he was in the dispensary in agony with an inflection that had been aggravated by the repeated soakings. He was to be "out of action" for at least a week the medics said.

Later that day, my unit was alerted for deployment to the Vietnamese-Cambodian border to block the infiltration of a North Vietnamese battalion that had apparently come by ship to a harbor in neutral Cambodia fifty miles from the border. I quickly packed my rucksack, drew maps of the area, and joined my unit in a combat assault by helicopter, expecting to be back in Sa Dec in, at most, a week's time.

Well, that's not how things worked out. Severe rains and wind reduced aviation support, both fixed-wing and choppers to almost zero, and we spent the next twenty-seven days engaged on and across the border with a fully manned, healthy, and well equipped NVA battalion in classic infantry to infantry combat. Our casualties were evacuated by boat and we got some resupply, but clearly that was not the case for our adversary, because on the morning of the twenty-seventh day, they were nowhere to be found, probably having run out of food, ammunition, and even the will to fight, and the sun had come out, meaning air support would be coming.

A flight of Huey's came in bringing resupply and my replacement, who reminded me (if I had really needed reminding), that I was scheduled to fly out of Ton Son Nut airbase near Saigon that very afternoon. I briefed him on the situation which he had monitored from "the rear," and he told me all my clothing and personal gear had been shipped to the States. I said my good byes to those I had served with and expressed my thanks for all they had shared with me. Dai Uy My shook my hand and gave me maybe the best compliment I have ever received. He said "I have been glad while you have been here."

I climbed on a chopper with open doors and flew to Saigon in the same set of jungle fatigues I had been in for twenty-seven days, soaked most of the time, and as was our routine, not wearing any underwear or socks (they only rotted). On arrival, I had only three hours to out-process (normally took two days), but it was remarkable how fast people wanted to move me on, as I finally realized how bad I stunk!

After a final Military Police check point (where the MP confiscated my K-Bar knife purchased in Gainesville, Florida, asserting it was "government property"), I boarded my "freedom bird" as the last passenger only to be told by the stewardess "You, sit in the back of the plane." And that is where I remained through stops in Japan and Hawaii, until Travis Air Force Base outside of San Francisco.

As the last passenger off the plane, I was greeted by an Air Force Technical Sergeant who said "Captain, you look like you could use a shower. Come with me." He took me to a crew billet and said "Put your stuff in two piles, the stuff you want me to wash and the stuff you want me to burn." I only had my rucksack, poncho liner, hammock, black peasant pants and shirt, a dirty uniform, and some paperwork so the choices were easy. I wanted to keep everything.

I said "Sergeant, clearly no one is going to let me fly across the US in my jungle fatigues."

"Don't worry, sir. Take a shower and relax. I'll be back in a half hour."

And, he was good to his word. I repacked my now clean gear in my clean rucksack and put on the complete Class B khaki uniform from shoes to hat he had found for me, the only thing missing was a plastic name tag. "Stuff from the Lost and Found," he remarked, then he urged, "Don't go out the front gate, that's where the protesters are. I'll drive you to the back gate where we have special cabs that will get you to the airport."

I thanked him again and he said, "Hey sir, my last day in service is tomorrow and I never had to go the Vietnam. I have been taking care of guys like you for the last six months. It's just the right thing to do."

When I got to the airport, no one accosted me, and I boarded my flight to Florida only to discover that my seat mate (two sets on each side in the 707 of the day) was the hippest hippy I had ever seen. Oh no, I thought. This is early November 1969, and I'm about to be blamed for everything. The guy in the window seat looked up and asked "Just get back, Captain?" I nodded, and he put out his hand and said, "I got back six months ago. Served as an infantry squad leader in the Central Highlands."

We spent the entire flight across America, or, across *The World*, to us veterans, sharing truly silly stories of which we both had plenty, and keeping many of the other passengers in stiches, as the stewardess kept giving us drinks. Welcome Home! Once again, I was simply lucky.

Our video in the Quonset hut is a set of narratives of personal experiences matched to combat footage. It ends with a tribute to Vietnam veterans showing a series of personal photographs, first of some of us as we were in the 1960s and early 70s, and then recently as Patriots Point volunteers. The narrator mentions that many served, and some died in this often misunderstood war that is now being reconsidered. As a family of four emerged from the theater, the mother asked me if her daughter, who had just seen my picture, could ask me a question. I love kid's questions and so I smiled at this seven-year-old, who looked me in the eye and asked in a clear voice, "Why didn't you die in Vietnam?"

Everyone within earshot was suddenly silent. As I got down on my knee, I said "Because I was lucky. Many weren't, but I was." Then I went on to tell her one of my "lucky stories," as many others listened in:

"I was walking along a paddy dike with the command group of my Vietnamese battalion, right behind the commander whose name was Captain My. It had been raining and the dike was muddy. The rice paddies on each side of the dike were about three feet lower down. Our troops were moving into a wood-line about fifty yards ahead of us.

Along with the rest of my field gear, the radio I was carrying weighed nearly thirty pounds, and its shoulder strap had shifted. When I tried to adjust it, my foot slipped in the mud and I started to fall sideways. Without thinking, I reached out for Captain My (who maybe weighed 110 pounds), and only succeeded in knocking both of us off the dike.

As we hit the water in the rice paddy, the dike where we had just been walking exploded. It was a booby-trapped artillery shell, set off by someone in the wood-line. Captain My was an expert in spotting booby traps and he had taught me to do the same, so when we stood up both a bit hard of hearing, he patted me on the back enthusiastically yelling that I had spotted the trap and saved our lives. I protested that I had only slipped and knocked him off by mistake, but he ignored me. Fortunately, no one was seriously injured by this explosion, but a few weeks later, I was surprised with the award of a Vietnamese Cross of Gallantry for my actions that muddy day. You see, young lady, sometimes it just OK to be lucky." This young visitor thanked me for sharing. Some days we just do the right thing.

Military service is risky even during peacetime. Accidents happen and people do dumb things. I've done my share including rock climbing without safety ropes or a partner. But travelling in helicopters seems to stand out as just plain risky. Some personal examples:

Early in my tour in Vietnam, I was assigned duty as a top secret courier between IV Corps Advisory Headquarters in Can Tho and MACV Headquarters in Saigon flying back and forth in an unarmed light observation chopper piloted by a very experienced Chief Warrant Officer scout pilot who was bored being a "taxi driver."

On one mission, I was delayed at MACV and by the time I got to the airstrip, it was dusk and we were not supposed to fly after dark for a variety of reasons. But the officer's club at Can Tho had an all-girl Australian band scheduled for that evening, and my pilot (and I admit me too) really wanted to see the show. So against policy, we took off and followed the main road south into the Delta.

It was nearly dark when we spotted a large convoy of fuel and ammunition trucks that were being ambushed. There were no other aircraft within visual range. The "old Scout" says "Captain, we've got to help."

My response seemed appropriate, "How? We're not armed." The old pilot says, "Oh, yes we are. You have your .45 and my .38 and I can make this bird sound like a machine-gun. So get shooting."

He rolled the OH-6 over the ambush site as I hung out the door emptying my pistol and then his. He did a tight role and we went down again as I fired my last clip.

Remarkably, the ambush broke. The firing stopped and the trucks rolled on. We gained altitude and made it back to Can Tho in time to see the show.

When I arrived at my temporary office at the IV Corps headquarters, I was told to report to the Chief of Staff immediately, which I did. Upon entering the Chief's office I found my pilot standing at rigid attention in front of an obviously angry colonel. I saluted and reported with my gut in turmoil. Had I killed my career by wanting to see that show?

After a long minute, the Chief spoke:

"I really don't know what to do with you two. Mister, you should lose your flight rating. You, Captain, should lose your security clearance. You two realize that you not only violated policy, but you put that packet of classified documents you were carrying at risk. I should court martial you both.

"But," he continued, "You saved Uncle Sam a bunch of valuable fuel, ammo, trucks and drivers, so, I'd also have to recommend you both for Air Medals with Vs for valor."

"Well, I can't do both, so I can't do either. Here!"

The Chief of Staff reached out with both hands, each holding a silver Zippo lighter. Mine was engraved on one side with "Killer" above "Can Tho, RVN 68-69."

"Captain, there was a gangster in the 1930s called "Killer Kane" who was a wiz with pistols. It seems to fit. Now both of you get outta here and don't do something that dumb again."

★★★

Later in my tour, my Vietnamese battalion was making a helicopter move into what was supposed to be a quiet landing zone. As was my habit during combat assaults, I sat on the floor of the chopper in the doorway with my feet on the skids so I could quickly exit the aircraft. Just as we touched down, a VC or NVA soldier popped up from a spider hole less than fifteen feet from the aircraft and fired a B-40 rocket launcher. The RPG round with propulsion flame still gushing flew right past my helmet, scorching the helmet cover and missing everyone on board, exited the other door. The surprised door gunner on our chopper fired too late, missing the fleeing VC. A bit of dumb luck for lots of us.

★★★

From fall of 1966 to spring of 1968, prior to my tour in Vietnam, I served with the 3rd Battalion, 51st Infantry (Mechanized) in the 2nd Brigade of the 4th Armored Division, stationed at a base outside of the lovely city of Erlangen near Nurnberg, not far from the West German border to the east.

I had only been on base for about a week when an order came down for me to be the Officer-In-Charge of a special resupply operation. Completely in the dark, I reported to the brigade S-4 (logistics staff officer) who filled me in. The French had decided to withdraw from

NATO and we Americans had lots of supply depots that had to be emptied ASAP (as soon as possible). I was to lead a convoy consisting of every supply truck in the brigade to a depot that was reportedly filled with repair parts for our armored vehicles, weapons, and communication gear, plus new items of equipment we were authorized to have as replacements for our stuff that was wearing out. My instructions were to "liberate" anything and everything we could use. Just fill up the trucks and get back here as fast as I could.

Supply in forward deployed units in Germany was tight due to the build-up in Vietnam, so this adventure had both symbolic and practical meaning for all of us. The drive west took nearly a full day. We crossed into France without incident and found the depot staffed with only a disinterested small guard force. We slept about five hours in the cabs of our trucks and then began to load boxes and crates, barrels and whole pieces of equipment, still in shipping packets, very early in the morning.

I'm pretty sure the noise we made didn't please the locals, but since the stuff was ours, we really didn't care. We knew that we were on a tight schedule imposed by the French, as well as expecting other American units to show up before long. So this was simply a "grab and go" operation.

The highlight of the trip was crossing the border from France back into Germany. I had heard the story of an American veteran of the D-Day landing in Normandy being hassled, years later by a French customs agent when the American was slow in pulling out his passport. In response to the agent's curt challenge, the GI stated with dignity "No one asked me for my passport when I landed here in 1944."

Like that passport agent, the customs control team at the border demanded a manifest of all we were carrying. As the Second Lieutenant, Officer-In-Charge, I informed the agent he could make his own manifest if he wanted to unload all the trucks, because I did not have one and had no intention of making one. I really had no idea what was on my twenty trucks.

My troops and I were unarmed, but we were tired and impatient, so I guess we looked like trouble. The agent gave me "one of those looks" and waved us through. Mission accomplished.

One of the rotating duties assigned to units in my brigade at Erlangen was the guarding of a "Special Weapon's Site," which we all knew, or at least believed, held nuclear artillery rounds and demolitions. The site was nearly an acre in size, surrounded by two chain-link fences topped with barbed-wire, enclosing concrete and dirt bunkers with steel doors and a command post and bunk-house combination. The site was on the edge of our local training area, at least three miles from the main post with access on a dirt tank trail.

When my platoon's turn came to serve a week as guards for this site, I was carefully briefed on my responsibilities and the standards of conduct that my soldiers and I would adhere to. I read and re-read the set of operating instructions, noting, in particular, that as Officer-of-the Guard, I had the authority to employ lethal force under certain conditions, including the breech of the outer fence line. I had both FM radio and land-line communication with the brigade headquarters.

I had twenty-six soldiers and four NCO's assigned to this platoon. We were armed with M-14 rifles, two M-60 machine guns and two grenade launchers. On site the first day, I was required to inventory and verify the live ammunition stored at the site, including CS tear gas canisters, and was reminded of the restrictions in place concerning the loading of weapons. By SOP (Standing Operating Procedures), we each loaded our rifle magazines with live ammunition and placed them in the lock box along with the other ammunition.

With my platoon sergeant guidance, we set up rotating guard duties and conducted required drills, practicing how we would defend the site. Actually, none of us ever expected to have to do this for real, but we trained just in case. We would defend from inside the inner fence. I also conducted some other training like first aid, protective masking drills, vehicle identification, and communication authentication procedures. And so our week moved along.

Around 2200 hours (10:00 pm) on our fourth day, the soldier in one of the observation posts atop a bunker, called down to report that he saw lights coming down the paved road from the nearest built up area that did not look like headlights, more like torches. I climbed up with my binoculars (we did not have a night vision device on site) and clearly there were people moving towards us. Soon we could hear the chanting of what now appeared to be a mob of anti-war or anti-nuclear protesters.

Scrambling down, I alerted those not currently on duty. The squad leaders quickly positioned their men as we had rehearsed, while I reported to brigade headquarters. The duty officer said he would call the German authorities and reminded me to follow procedures rigidly. By this time, the mob, and it really was a mob of close to one-hundred people, was only fifty yards from the outer fence. I ordered my NCOs to draw ammunition, and have their soldiers load their weapons, but keep them on safe and the barrels elevated. I picked up two CS canisters and ordered everyone to be ready to put on protective masks which we carried in cases on our hips. The rule – non-lethal force first.

Someone from the mob threw a torch toward the outer fence which sparked harmlessly. Just then the sound of German police sirens reached us and soon a full squad of officers armed with clubs and batons charged into the mob, which quickly dispersed. After a few tense minutes, the senior police officer approached the outer gate where I met him. He asked "Is all secure?" "Yes!" I assured him. Then he looked me in the eye and inquired, "Would you have fired on the crowd?" I responded,

"Yes, I would have if they had breached the outer fence." He nodded. "Good. Have a quiet evening," and walked away.

I've often wondered if I really would have ordered my soldiers to fire and if I would have done so myself. I know I would have used the tear gas first, then—who knows.

★★★

One final helicopter story about *someone else* doing something dumb. I was serving as the S-3 Operations and Training staff officer for 1st Brigade, 1st Division (Mechanized) in the early 1980s. My unit deployed from Ft. Riley, Kansas to southern Germany to participate in a REFORGER (Return of Forces to Germany) field exercise. The "Devil's Brigade" as we were nicknamed was attached to the German 5th Panzer Grenadier Division for combined arms training in the Black Forest area. Our "adversary" was a unit of Canadian mechanized infantry.

During the final day of maneuvers, I was flying in a light observation helicopter, an OH-58, observing the movement of two of the brigade's battalions on a sweep operation intended to outflank the Canadian defensive positions. According to standard operating procedures and flight rules, we were flying "nap of the earth," low level flight well below where the "fast movers," US Air Force close air support aircraft, were supposed to operate.

We were climbing out of a valley nearing a grass covered hill-top when an A-10 Attack Aircraft shot passed us, not more than a hundred feet above. If we had crested the hill one second sooner, we would have collided. As it was, the shock wave of the jet's passing slammed us into the ground. Somehow, the pilot maintained control of the OH-58 as we bounced back into the air. The pilot and I looked at each other, shook our heads and remarked simultaneously, "Did you get the number of that bus?"

In military operations as in the rest of life, there are rules that make sense, that are needed and must be followed, or someone is likely to get hurt. We never found out if the A-10 pilot even saw us, and we chose not to report the incident. The tactical exercise ended successfully with no major maneuver damage, no accidental casualties, and no hard feelings among allies.

My twenty-six year career as a soldier was filled with experiences and people who simply made life worth living. I understood my mission and believed in the oath I had taken when accepting the honor of a commission in the United States Army. And, I still do!

CHAPTER 9

This chapter has been omitted due to the untimely death of Dick West. He will be discussed later in the acknowledgement portion of this publication.

CHAPTER 10

VOLUNTEER CLAUDE ROUNTREE

★★★

Claude Rountree: Photo property of *Scuttlebutt*

The following information was obtained from Claude in response to requests to provide some information about him for inclusion in the anthology *Short Rations From Patriots Point Volunteers*. It is utilized with permission of Claude, the author of the article, and Chip Biernbaum, the editor of *Scuttlebutt: Voice of the Patriots Point Volunteers*. Spring 2017 edition:

Claude was born in Charleston, SC. He graduated from the Citadel in 1971 with a BA in English, and Webster University in 1999 with an MA in Computer Resources and Information Management. He worked as a US Army transportation officer from August 1971, until his retirement from the service in March 1995. While in the military, over the course of his twenty-four years, he served in various leadership and staff positions at such places as Frankfurt, Germany; Charleston AFB, SC; Bettembourg, Luxembourg; Military Ocean Terminal, Sunny Point, NC; and Stuttgart, Germany, just to name a few. He also supported such operations as "Just Cause" (Panama), and "Desert Storm" and "Desert Shield" (Iraq).

Claude shares the following: *I was born and served during the Cold War (1948-199), so I don't think it's far-fetched to think of anyone during this time period.as a 'cold-war soldier.' My 'battlefields' were wherever in the world I served: from SMLM (Soviet Military Liaison Mission) vehicles scouting our convoys throughout Germany, to meetings with high ranking Warsaw-Pact officers in Bulgaria, Hungary, Poland, Albania, or Czechoslovakia, demonstrating how the military can operate in a democratic society. It was all part of the dance we called the Cold War, which was won by the NATO countries, as witnessed by the fall of the Berlin Wall in 1989 and the dissolution of the Eastern Bloc countries.*

While stationed at the US European Command (EUCOM) in Stuttgart, Germany, I was part of the initial eight-person Military-to-Military Contact Team sanctioned by the State Department which established contacts with the former Eastern Bloc countries. Contacts were established through the State Department and US embassies to foster better relationships and to promote the democratic way of life. I participated in military-to-military discussions in Czechoslovakia, Hungary, Bulgaria, Albania and Poland, ultimately becoming the Polish Desk Officer, establishing an in-country, four-person US team at the Minister of Defense in Warsaw, Poland. These efforts continue today and were instrumental in establishment of the George C. Marshall European Center for Security Studies based in Garmisch-Partenkirchen, Germany, whose mission is, to create a more stable security environment by advancing democratic institutions and relationships; promoting active, peaceful, whole-of-government approaches to address transnational and regional security challenges; and creating and enhancing enduring partnerships worldwide.

Also, while at EUCOM, I was responsible for the transfer of US combat equipment to our NATO partners as a consequence of the Conventional Armed Forces in Europe (CFE) Treaty between NATO and the former Warsaw Pact, which established comprehensive limits on key categories of conventional military equipment in Europe. This involved establishing transfer requirements, such as where, how and who is to receive materials, to include maintenance standards, which of course differed from country to country. Due to past unstable relationships between some countries, maintenance team visit dates did not coincide! Since my boss was an Army three-star, I never had a problem hitching a helicopter ride wherever and whenever I needed to go.

My favorite job was as the Commander of the General Support Center BENELUX (GSCB) in the country of Luxembourg, where I was responsible for maintaining the European Theater's ten-day wartime resupply, ranging from tanks to the European pipeline, stored in humidity-controlled warehouses in Luxembourg, Belgium, and the Netherlands. I had a military and civilian staff monitoring a contractor workforce upwards of 800 personnel. My secretary spoke French, German, English, and the Luxembourg language. Thank goodness I spoke English! My Luxembourgers always called me the "coach" because I managed by "walking around" and giving pep talks. During my time there, we hosted the very first visit of the Grand Duke of Luxembourg, at the time Grand Duke Jean. The Luxembourgers were so proud and loved Americans due to our liberating their country during World War II. In fact, General "Georgie" Patton is buried in the American Military Cemetery in Luxembourg."

Claude retired in 1995 at the United Sates Transportation Command (USTRANSCOM) at Scott Air Force Base, Illinois, as a Lieutenant Colonel. After retirement from the Army, he worked for a variety of companies in the information technology field, primarily focused on transportation technical solutions and systems. He picks up the story: *After retiring, we remained in Illinois, where I worked as a defense contractor (with Systems Research and Applications, Inc., Unisys Corporation and the Dynamic Research Corporation) for USTRANSCOM until 2006, when we accepted a job with a company (GeoLogics Corporation) working at SPAWAR in Charleston. We had finally come home! My wife is a North Charleston girl. After a brief stint from 2013 to 2015 as a systems analyst for Systems Research and Applications in Scott Air Force Base in Illinois, I took a position as a project analyst for Tapestry Solutions, a Boeing Company, in the U.S. Navy TacMobile program supporting the Maritime Patrol and Reconnaissance Force (MPFR), which flies P-8 Poseidon and P-3 Orion airplanes.*

Claude and Theresa were married in The Citadel Chapel on January 29, 1972, right after he completed his military training at the Motor Officer Automotive Course (MOAC) at Ft. Knox, KY. As Claude shares: *It was a commute of twelve-hours through the mountains before the interstate was completed – true love!* They have three children. Susan Driggers is married to Jon Driggers. They have two daughters (Lauren and Emmy) and live in Banner Elk, NC. Daniel Rountree is married to Catherine-Alexa. They have two daughters (Cousteau and Kepler) and live in Charlotte, NC. Claude and Theresa's daughter, Laura Rountree, lives in Chicago.

Claude has some hobbies: woodworking, reading military history, and golf. He does not volunteer for any other organizations other than their church, Christ our King in Mt. Pleasant. He became a Patriots Point volunteer in January 2016.

Claude has a final comment: *Since I began volunteering at Patriots Point, I have felt a sense of camaraderie and pride. I am constantly buoyed by the enthusiastic responses by visitors . . . proud to be an American! The Patriots Point volunteers and staff make it so! As I walk up to the "Fighting Lady" whenever it's my shift, all my troubles just lift away. It's a great place to be and to volunteer.*

CHAPTER 11

VOLUNTEER RALPH STONEY BATES, SR.

★★★

CID Officer, Ralph Stoney Bates, on Monkey Mountain, near DaNang, Vietnam, 1968
Photo property of author

For the first seventeen years of my life, I responded to the name Stoney, my middle name. When I entered the Marine Corps, I responded to Ralph, because the Marine Corps didn't recognize middle names, though, sometimes, some people would still use my middle name to address me. Since I began writing books, people I came in contact with began to address me as Stoney. I guess it sounds more literary-like. Anyway, I prefer to use my middle name, again.

My birthplace is Anniston, Alabama. It is also my wife's birthplace. I grew up in Anniston until my mother died in 1948. I was ten-years-old. After that, I lived in New Orleans, LaGrange, GA, Alva, OK, and back to Anniston where I entered the Marines. I was seventeen-years-old. By the time I turned twenty, I had completed boot camp, infantry training, various technical schools, served eighteen months duty in the Orient, been involved in a multi-national amphibious landing exercise titled "Operation Strongback," in the Philippines, and met the girl who would become my wife; Lyn. We married in 1959, while I was a Drill Instructor at Parris Island. Lyn and I have been married sixty years as this writing is published. She was, and still is a Marine wife. Together, we moved twenty-two times with the Marines, and ten times since retiring from the Marines. We continue to lead a nomadic lifestyle. It's just the way we are.

Like many before me, and many more who will follow me, the Marine Corps is the foundation of my adult life. After serving twenty-six-years active duty, I continue to serve the Marine Corps in numerous other ways. Writing and publishing books and articles is one of those ways. Having authored three and a half books and three Marine Corps Gazette articles about Marine Corps legends and lifestyle, I continue with this, my second anthology, about the volunteers at the Naval and Maritime Museum of Patriots Point. Many of these authors also describe their military service as a foundation of their adult lives.

My Marine Corps career took me from an enlisted man (private to sergeant) into the officer ranks, via the warrant officer route. I have held military occupational skills in aviation, infantry, drill instructor, criminal investigation, corrections, and military police. Much of my duties during my career involved teaching, or instructing. Rather than identifying all the instructor titles, let me just stipulate that there were many.

Later, I even became an adjunct or part-time college and university level instructor at various colleges and universities. Instructing others has been my forte for much of my career.

I have served with some of the finest men and women on the face of this earth, and also a few, thankfully very few, flaming asses who somehow thought they were the finest men and women on this earth. Likewise, in my law enforcement career—ditto! People are people. Character and reputation are not always synonymous.

One of my most enjoyable duties was as an instructor at the US Army Military Police School at Ft Gordon, GA. One of the most challenging was as the Provost Marshal of Camp Butler, Okinawa. The most career-enhancing was my deployment to the combat zone in Vietnam where I was the Officer-In-Charge of a Criminal Investigations Department for the 1st Marine Air Wing and the commander of a composite rifle company (composed mostly of Tango Security Marines) during the 1968 TET Offensive. My toughest duty was that of a Drill Instructor at Parris Island. The most tranquil duty was as the executive officer of Range Company, Camp Fuji (on the side of a volcano by the same name), Japan. The most memorable was as a young military policeman in the MAG-11, MABS-11 Guard at the Naval Air Station, Atsugi, Japan. It was at that location, I became involved in the apprehension of and "chaser" (as in prisoner chaser) of Private Lee Harvey Oswald, USMC. You got to read "The Uncanny Wisdom of Marine First Sergeants," the first chapter of *Short Rations For Marines.*

My Marine Corps career was excellent, and my civilian law enforcement career was good. I never had any victory laps, or high accolades as a Marine or as a law enforcement officer (deputy sheriff). Like most Marines and law enforcement types, there were those peaks (great successes), and there were those, as the Irish would say: *oh, shite* "valleys" along most career paths. Most of the time, in both of my careers, I managed to get to the peaks often, with some occasional trips into the valleys. Every now and then, it was into those miserably deep valleys.

Regardless of being on the high ones, or in the deep ones, I managed to accomplish any mission delegated to, or assumed by me, throughout my careers. Also, I increased my formal academic education from high-school drop-out to earning a Bachelor of Science (Summa Cum Laude), in Criminology at Sam Houston State University, followed by some graduate credits. Also, I attended and completed the FBIs National Academy (124th Session), at Quantico, VA, and being selected for promotion to lieutenant colonel of Marines (which I did not accept as I had selected to retire). I'm retired from both the Marine Corps, and later retired as a deputy sheriff, knowing that I had given my best efforts in all my duties and responsibilities, upheld the honor of my Marine Corps, and provided honest, diligent support to my Corps, my county sheriff (as a deputy sheriff), and to my country.

I'll relate just a few examples: While stationed at Fort Gordon, which might be exemplified by the words of SLA Marshall's famous statement about the 4th Marine Brigade in France with the American Expeditionary Forces in 1918, . . . *they are like a life raft of leathernecks in an ocean of soldiers.* So stated Marshall. There was only a handful of Marines at the US Army's Military Police School, yet we were treated very well by everyone on that Post. Marine Colonel Archie Van Winkle (MOH Recipient) was my de facto "boss," from Headquarters Marine Corps, although I reported directly to Army Major Claude Owen at the Military Police School. When I arrived in the late summer of 1970, the military police school had not been alerted to the pending arrival of thousands of Marines for training. We had much to do and little time to do it, but it was done.

"Arch" visited us several times at Ft Gordon, as he did earlier when we were stationed at Parris Island where I was Brig Officer. He was our principle speaker for our Marine Corps birthday event at Fort Gordon.

It was attended by Army personnel, as well as Marines. It became the social event of the year. Also, Lyn was the chairperson of the major charity fund-raising event of the Army Officer's Wives Club, and received accolades from the Army command upon our departure for her work. Our time with the Army was a highlight of our time in the Corps. Thousands of Marines were trained in corrections, investigations, and military police duties while we were stationed with the Army. It was rewarding to be in on the ground floor with the military police/corrections/criminal investigations occupational specialty. And, it was rewarding to have been assigned "other service" duty as a Marine. I received the Army Commendation Medal award. One of my peaks!

Later, after my unaccompanied assignment at tranquil, beautiful, and exotic Camp Fuji, Japan, I was transferred to Camp Butler, Okinawa as deputy provost marshal working for the legendary Stanley J. Wawrzyniak. Stan was assigned as provost marshal of Camp Butler, Okinawa. Although Stan was a lieutenant colonel and the provost marshal billet was that of a colonel's rank, his reputation, and brashness solidified his position. Just three months into my assignment, right after my wife paid me a visit from the States, our commanding general, appointed me, a major, as the Provost Marshal of Camp Butler. Stan was assigned as commanding officer of Headquarters Battalion while awaiting orders back to the States and a well-earned retirement.

Now, understand this, I was certainly no Stan Wawrzyniak. I didn't chew tobacco, didn't wear a Navy Cross, wasn't a WW II, Korean War, and Vietnam War veteran, didn't have a reputation as a "hell-fighting, devil-may-care Marine," and didn't leave a wet, sloppy "chaw" on the general's secretary's desk each time while visiting the general (she would cover it with tissue until Stan emerged to retrieve his "chaw" lump.) Stan was all that, and more. Yes, I was a far-cry from this legendary devil-may-care Lieutenant Colonel Stan Wawrzyniak. But, Suddenly—I am THE Provost Marshal of the largest military police unit in the Marine Corps.

Immediately, my big challenge came from full-bird colonels who felt they should be THE provost marshal, and proceeded in various direct and indirect methods to oust me from my position. I faced those challenges, with a little bit of help from other sources. Let's just say that having strong support from your boss and having excellent relations with the Japanese National Police, plus giving top-notch performance in supporting your boss, gives one a unique advantage.

My military police and criminal investigators were also top-notch performers. The general gave me and my department many unique missions. One in particular was to provide security for the extraction of Marine Private First Class Robert Garwood (the deserter and collaborator) from Vietnam. It was around March 1979, that representatives from the United States Department of State met in the general's office. I was present at that meeting. Seven years after US forces were withdrawn from Vietnam, four years after the fall of the Republic of Vietnam to the communist, a *captured* Marine wanted to come home.

After that meeting, I selected a detail of my men, drew hand-held radios for each, equipped them with shoulder holsters for their assigned .45 auto pistols, trained them in drawing and firing from concealed (under the shirt) positions, outlined a comprehensive security plan consistent with the use of deadly force, which had been authorized, and rehearsed various action and reaction procedures. By the time the target (Garwood) arrived via C-130 from Bangkok, we were ready.

We got him from the landing of the aircraft at Fatima's airstrip, to Kue hospital, where we kept him with limited access for several days, while he was positively identified via fingerprints and dental records. He was given a physical exam and maintained in total isolation. Then, we set up a ruse to get him from Okinawa into confinement at Great Lakes. While the world-wide media concentrated on, what they initially thought was the evacuation of the Shah of Iran being conducted, but later discovered it was a Marine deserter from the Vietnam War who had perhaps served in combat with the enemy against Americans, they were in a frenzied drive for information and access. Both were denied. When we were set to move Garwood, they followed our Garwood look-alike, meandering from the hospital to Kadena Air Force Base, while two of my CID men along with an undercover escort, departed for the Naha Airport to board a North-West Orient Airline's flight to Chicago with Garwood in tow and cuffs. Mission accomplished.

I remembered the Garwood case intimately. As the officer-in-charge of the CID (criminal investigation department) in Vietnam, we had "salt-and-pepper" reports periodically. That was a black man and a white man who appeared to be leading attacks against Marine forces in combat. Thus they were named, "salt and pepper." I am convinced to this day that Garwood was the "salt." He was courts martialed at Camp Lejeune.

Interestingly, about a year after the Garwood event, I got into one of those valleys by conducting a rather sensitive investigation at the request of my boss. Without disclosing too much, let us just say that it was a domestic incident type investigation. The investigation was conducted professionally and in a quasi-clandestine manner. I was pleased with the results, and so was my boss. The unexpected problem arose when the commander of one of the two subjects of the investigation felt I had overstepped my bounds. He was NOT pleased with the results of the investigation. My boss was pleased, but this other boss was not. When I delivered my CID report to him, I took an ass-chewing par-*excellance*! It was the first time I had been in trouble for doing my job.

After that humbling experience, I reported back to my real boss. No sweat! As expected, my boss supported me completely, without any dissention. I was assured: Everything would be fine. Then, the unexpected happened.

As a result of orders from Headquarters Marine Corps, these two commanders changed positions. The "not pleased with the results of the investigation," became my actual boss.

Even with the change, I seemed to be still doing fine, when, out-of-the-blue, a report came in that we (the Marines) were missing some M-72 LAW's, an anti-tank weapon, from an ammo bunker located in one of our camps.

Several separate issues began to merge. First, the International Economic Summit was convening in Tokyo, Japan. Second, the terrorist group, Japanese Red Army, had been active in Japan, and a cadre was supposedly on Okinawa. Third, President Jimmy Carter was attending the Summit and was airborne on his way to Tokyo. Fourth, a LAW can take down an aircraft with a lucky shot. Fifth, someone had fired a rocket, believed to be home-made, at the Imperial Palace in Tokyo, and, sixth and last, was the treaty referred to as the Status of Forces Agreement (SOFA) between Japan and the United States; it stipulated that this type of an event must be reported to the Japanese National Police. I was the one who would normally report this event; however, I was ordered by my new boss, not to report the event. I was in a quandary. The worst case scenario flashed by my psyche: *US President's aircraft downed by missile approaching landing in Tokyo.* I shook that thought outta my mind only to have it reenter, again, and again.

I sought advice from several trusted sources; however, the only sound advice received was: "You should ask your boss to put it in writing." That didn't go over very well with my boss! Another piece of *advice* was—"You're in a hell of a mess," and, "Wouldn't want to be in your shoes." I contemplated everything from resigning my commission to defying an order.

Just as I had finished making a decision, and contemplating the end of my Marine Corps career in inglorious fashion, my interpreter/cultural affairs officer, a Japanese National, entered my office telling me that the Chief of the Prefectural Police was on the phone inquiring about the missing weapons. The Japanese National Police were aware of the incident. And, I didn't do it!!

I did find out later that when the weapons were discovered missing, the Japanese security guard assigned to the weapons storage area of the missing weapons, had reported that fact to my Japanese Security Guard Commander. That commander, hearing of my difficult situation, discussed it with the interpreter/cultural affairs person, and he notified the Prefectural Police.

Wait! It's not over. A few weeks, or maybe a couple of months later, a lieutenant colonel reported to Camp Butler, and was assigned to duty as THE Provost Marshal of Camp Butler. I was reassigned as deputy provost marshal. As the new provost marshal was adjusting to the job, my office was moved to the basement of the military police building. I was isolated from the staff of the provost marshal's office. I knew if I remained in that basement office, other *shoes* would *drop.* I went into the office at midnight one night, picked up the phone, and called Security and Law Enforcement Branch at Headquarters Marine Corps. Upon getting access to the Director, my first words were, "Get me out of here!!" I stated loud and forcefully to the Head of Security and Law Enforcement. "Start packing! I'll have your orders cut at once," was the thankful reply.

Making a long enough story as short as possible, I became the Provost Marshal of the Marine Corps Air-Ground Combat Center, Twenty-nine Palms, California. My wife and I sat together at our dinner table, as my twenty-sixth-year of Marine Corps service began. We began to discuss our future within the ranks of the Marine Corps. As usual there was the plus column and the minus column on the paper tablet before us. Clearly the various incidences as Provost Marshal confronting seniors, the LAW incident, my hasty departure from the basement in Okinawa, and even my Criminal Investigation Officer assignment years earlier, wherein I caused career changes in a few senior (to me) officers, told me that the sun was setting on my Marine Corps career. We began to discuss retirement from our beloved Marine Corps. It was a strained discussion but we both reached the same conclusion. For example, I knew I would not be selected for lieutenant colonel.

Surprisingly, I was selected for, attended, and completed the 124th Session of the FBI National Academy at Quantico, and attended the US Air Force Security Police Officer Advanced Course at the Lackland Air Force Base; even with that done, I felt I was not going any higher in rank.

While at the FBI National Academy, I interviewed for a position with a sheriff's office. I thought nothing would come of it. But, my wife and I began to make plans for life after the Marine Corps. Resumes were being dispatched to dozens of locations, when out-of-the-blue; I'm offered a position with that New York Sheriff's Office; whereupon, I placed my request for retirement into motion.

To my total surprise, indeed complete shock, I was selected for promotion to lieutenant colonel. It was tempting, but the die had been cast.

One of the most rewarding events of my Marine Corps career occurred a few weeks before we departed for retirement. A knock on my door at our quarters was answered to find our commanding general standing there. "Got a beer"? he asked.

We sat in lounge chairs in my back yard, enjoying a beer, looking at the San Jacinto Mountains in the distance towering over Palm Springs down in the other end of the Morongo Valley, sipping our beer, and chatting. It was a typical June day in the high desert, about 120 degrees in the sun. Cool in the shade of our umbrella. It was an honor for me to have my commanding general, in this setting, ask me to reconsider my decision to retire. He was almost persuasive. I felt awed by the simplicity and directness of it all. He could have had me report to his office. He could have asked the chief of staff to talk to me. Instead, it was one of those peaks.

As we finished our beers, we walked back through the quarters to the front door. He stepped out, stood for a second or two as his driver started his staff car, turned to me, and extended his hand. "Good luck, Ralph!" he said.

"Thank you, sir," was all I could think of to reply.

He turned to leave. Then, suddenly turned again and faced me. In that instant, I felt it was to relate to me something he had bottled up inside him and he needed to get it out now. "Ralph," he stated, looking directly into my eyes. "You did the right thing in Okinawa. What you did, and how you did it, is what caused you to be selected for lieutenant colonel. Think about it, major. If you change your mind," he hesitated, "You know where to find me." He turned and walked to his staff car, and waved as his driver drove away.

That event on my front porch was my last peak as an active duty Marine. It was a pretty high one.

A few weeks later my approval for retirement came in. I skipped the quarterly parade. We quietly departed our Corp while at the top of that peak, and slid into the ranks of Marine, (Retired).

What is obvious from the outcome of this event on my front porch at 29 Palms, is that everyone in the Marine Corps believed that it was me who had notified the Japanese National Police. Until now, the true story has never been told.

★★★

At this point, in my story I will digress back fourteen years to another July day. My orders to Vietnam (FMF PAC, III MAF Ground) came in July 1967. I was assigned to the Camp Pendleton Base Brig as Security Officer at the time. I'd been there three years. My transfer to Staging Battalion came in August. And I, along with around 180 or so enlisted men, from private to first sergeant, began combat training. I ended up being the OIC of this replacement draft. My draft first sergeant was deploying to Vietnam for the second time so his son, currently in Vietnam, may return home. It was Marine Corps policy, then. Training was tough and necessary to have everyone departing for combat duty singing from the same sheet of music.

In those days, anyone living in on-base housing was told they had sixty days to vacate quarters. My wife and I found a house being built in a neighborhood outside the back gate, and we bought a home for her and our kids to stay while I participated in the *Southeast Asia War Games.* I was recently promoted to first lieutenant. Money was tight. But, we managed to close on the house just before I departed. It was on Elaine Avenue in Oceanside, California and was full of *single* wives and kids whose husbands were deployed. Casualty Assistance Officers accompanied by Chaplains roamed the neighborhoods daily in that dreaded Marine Corps sedan. Because our house was near the entrance, Lyn saw them every day. Tears still come to her eyes when we mention it.

Departure for a combat zone has been reenacted between millions of American males and females since the American Revolutionary War. Hundreds of thousands of boyfriends-girlfriends, husbands-wives, all react differently, with a sameness that is historical in content, yet, never choreographed. It was now our turn. It's never easy. It's an individual event, repeated with an awkward similarity. You do things and go places you've never got around to doing or going. You take dozens of "what if" photographs. "What if," he doesn't come back? It's the *got to have these photographs* type photographs. The usual promises are made, "I'll come home. I'll come back to you," with an uneasy feeling that many will not come back . . . alive. Some will never come back. Like wars before Vietnam; to this day, some have not returned from those wars. But, you put your "man-face" on and reassure all will be well—with you. Hopefully!

With your training still in high intensity, you suddenly are informed that your departure date has been stepped up. It is tomorrow, not next week. Lyn drives me to the Staging Battalion barracks where busses await boarding of my draft and me. We drive to Norton Airforce Base for departure to Okinawa. First stop for inbound Marines into Vietnam. There, we undergo more training. There, my orders are changed. I receive a change of orders from III MAF (Ground) to III MAF (Air). I'm to report to the First Marine Aircraft Wing.

As we prepared to depart for DaNang, my 1st Sergeant was informed of the death of his son—Killed in combat in Vietnam.

Upon arriving at DaNang Airbase, I'm met by a corporal who drives me to G-1 of the 1st MAW. There I receive notice that I am ordered to be the Officer-In-Charge of the Criminal Investigation Detachment (CID) replacing Fred Stilton. I have two investigators and a closet size office in an old French building. After all my training, including firing just about every infantry weapon in the Marine Corps arsenal, I'm issued a snub-nosed, five-shot, air-weight revolver with one box of .38 caliber ammunition. Hello! "Can't I get a bigger gun?" I asked. "Sir, this is the T/E (table of equipment) weapon for criminal investigators."

First thing I did was to prevail on a Navy Construction Battalion (Sea Bee's) to build me an office complete with evidence lockers, obtained a radio, jeep, and an administrative corporal and Vietnamese secretary/ interpreter. Next I visited the 1st MAW Group and Squadron (including LAAM Ban) commanders. This entailed travel either by helicopter and/or convoy. My first exposure to actual combat was when a convoy I had joined with one of my investigators on our way to a LAAMB

(Light Anti-aircraft Missile Battalion) on top of the Hai Van Pass, our convoy was ambushed. Scared would be an understatement. Laying in a ditch on the side of the road, holding a small, snub-nose revolver, while a bunch of infantry Marines blazed away at the ambushers with M-60 machine guns, M-16 rifles, M-79 grenade launchers, and 12 gauge shotguns firing *flechette* ammo. After it was over, I said to my investigator, "Tom, we gotta get bigger guns."

Eventually, we did get bigger guns, and more investigators, plus the CBs constructed a Southeast Asia style hut next to my office to accommodate living space for seven investigators and my admin clerk corporal. Together we filled sandbags and constructed two bunkers, one next to the office and the other next to the quarters of the investigators. These bunkers saved lives as incoming rockets of 120 and 140 millimeter were common and, over time, the sides of the bunkers were dotted with shrapnel holes.

In that war zone we pretty much threw away the rule book and did anything and everything we had to do in order to open, investigate, and close cases. We investigated things the FBI and/or the NIS (Naval Investigative Service) would normally take over, if we were in the United States. But, we were not in the United States. We were in a very hot war zone. We had numerous very interesting and very important cases. One in particular: I received a report from one of the squadron commanders that the pilots were firing missiles at targets only to have those missiles loop back toward the firing aircraft. Someone was tampering with those guidance systems. We worked and solved that case. Another: We received a report from a source that an *officer*, in a unit, was believed not to be an officer, but an imposter. They were right. He was a civilian who conned his way into Vietnam pretending to be a Marine Corps officer, He was a civilian nut-job who had tried to enlist, but was not acceptable, and managed to get a set of utilities, a lieutenant's rank insignia, someone else's orders, and made modifications to them. Apparently flew commercial to Okinawa, and "*joined* the Marines." I locked him up in the III MAF Brig and later placed him on a flight back to Okinawa. We had murders, robberies, rapes, and a couple of what could have been called treason cases. We had money laundering with military payment certificates, piasters, and US dollars changing hands, we worked big-time black-market cases, we had Viet Cong agents, ARVIN (Army of the Republic of Vietnam) troops shooting at US personnel, and the strange case of the Tech Rep.

Tech Reps (Technical Representatives) of aircraft, and other, manufactures providing civilian assistance to aviation squadrons, and other entities were common. One in particular came to our attention as a suspect stealing weapons from the PX on Hill 327 near the airbase and selling those weapons to the VC. We opened an investigation on this supposedly "civilian" and ultimately had him confined awaiting charges. A week or two later, my boss, Major General Norm Anderson called me to his office to get "briefed" on the case. His last words from that meeting: "Ralph, get this guy out of the brig. Place him on the next flight you can locate going to Okinawa. Don't ask any questions. Just do it!" My last words at that meeting were, "Aye, Aye, Sir!"

About two or three weeks later, I get a call from Air Force OSI (Office of Special Investigation) asking me to come visit them on the other side of the airbase. Arriving, they showed me a photo asking me if I knew who it was. I did. It was the same guy I had locked up, removed from confinement, and had him flown to Okinawa. I'll leave this story, at this point, in the classic lady or the tiger fashion. Remember that story from high-school readings? There are two doors. He (the main character) must open one of them. Behind one door is a hungry tiger. Behind the other door is a beautiful lady. The story ends with, "He opened the door."

I took over Tango Security, the security of the Marine Corps side of the DaNang airbase, while the assigned officer-in-charge went on his R&R. It was an additional duty. I was still OIC of CID. We were setting up a drug bust at a local hotel in DaNang, across the road from the ARVIN (Army of the Republic of Vietnam) I Corps Headquarters. At about 2230 that late 28th of January night, we had made the bust. Then, handcuffed and searched the suspects. And, we also confiscated drugs, money and weapons. We had the cuffed suspects on the ground in the parking lot, had secured the money, guns, and drugs into evidence bags, while awaiting a transport vehicle to take them to the brig. It was near 2300 when my staff-sergeant called my attention to the area across the road, at the ARVIN compound. I could see dark figures coming out of the river and moving toward the wall around the ARVIN headquarters. We were just across the road, no more than fifty-yards away from them. Suddenly, the half-naked bodies quickly went back into or at the edge of the river, just before a massive blast or two lit the area briefly, and the human figures rose from the river banks, I estimated at least half a hundred or so, bolted through the holes in the wall firing weapons and tossing more explosive charges. It was, for us, though I didn't realize it at the time, the start of the 1968 TET Offensive.

I had five or six men in custody, two or three lightly armed criminal investigators and two III MAF MPs borrowed from one of the Military Police Battalions armed with .45 caliber auto pistols. I told my sergeant to dump the drugs and money in the river, un-cuff the suspects, give them their weapons back with orders to return to their military unit, and my MPs and investigators jumped into our two jeeps and hightailed it back to the airbase. As we drove from DaNang City toward the airbase, rockets were lighting up the sky and impacting all around the airbase. We were driving faster than we should have, and the security police at the gate on the Air Force side of the airfield almost opened fire on us. It took us awhile, having to stop, dismount, and take cover a couple of times, before we arrived back at the Wing Headquarters compound. We could hear gunfire south of us and also more gunfire and explosions what appeared to be the direction of the Marine flight line. We had no idea what was going on except this night was alive with gunfire, rockets, and invisible aircraft above us. "Spooky" opened up, pouring its *molten lava* out of the dark skies, onto the entrance to Happy Valley, on some ground targets that appeared very close to the airbase. Needless to say, our pucker-factor was tight. Around 0100, I noticed a note on my desk to report to my C.O. immediately.

Immediately, became around 0600 the next day. I was told that I was to take some Tango Security personnel and some "volunteers," and move by truck toward the south of the airbase toward 3rd Tank Battalion. After much confusion in organizing and getting in transit, I finally got in place to prepare defensive positions. We were to defend a sector south of the airbase. Later that night we had some contact, a brief firefight broke out. Then a calm as the VC or NVA withdrew. Never did know who they were. We were in the field for a few days. We held our positions. We were probed a few times, tense at other times, and a nervous calm in between. We were later relieved by MPs from the MP Battalion, and I returned to command Tango Security around the perimeter of the Marine sector of the airbase. There, we got a few probes, a few firefights, and much boredom. When the OIC of Tango Security returned late from his R&R, I went back to full time CID duties. I thanked my lucky stars for the training I had received from all sources including Infantry Training at Camp Lejeune, after Boot Camp, The Basic School at Quantico, and the Staging Battalion combat training at Camp Pendleton, and Okinawa.

As our case-load grew, new CID personnel came into Vietnam, while others rotated back to the "land of the big PX." I had my R&R, and later, my relief came in. Tragically, he was killed in action a few weeks later. Much later, I rotated back to the States with orders to Camp Pendleton, which were modified while in Okinawa (a pattern develops) to report to Parris Island. I received a Navy Commendation Medal with Combat V at a parade at Parris Island. Another peak!

After my retirement from the Corps of Marines, I worked for that Sheriff's Department in Monroe County, New York. After four years as a sheriff's deputy-superintendent and two years as County Director of Emergency Preparedness, I began work for the Broward County (Florida) Sheriff's Office and retired (thankfully) after ten years as a sheriff's deputy. Most of those years were in defensive modes; however, that's, another story, at another time. After retiring from that sheriff's office, my wife and I eventually moved back to where we began our life together—South Carolina. *Nothing could be finer than to be in Carolina.*

I enjoy being a volunteer at Patriots Point. I continue to write, books, magazine articles, and newspaper opinion pieces sometimes appearing in the Charleston *Post and Courier* and *Moultrie News.* I am passionate about, and enjoy advocating for the National Medal of Honor Museum. Another tragic story, for another time.

Here at Patriots Point, one of my most memorable experiences was the subject of an Opinion Page article, written by me, appearing in the Charleston *Post and Courier* newspaper. I had just met two Medal of Honor recipients while on duty at *The Vietnam Experience*, got off duty, went home, picked up the newspaper and read where the City of Mt Pleasant Planning Commission had unanimously disapproved the plans to construct the National Medal of Honor Museum at Patriots Point in Mt Pleasant. The chairman was quoted as saying, "It was a little too much." I wondered why the commission and the museum folks didn't have conversations before this abrupt unanimous rejection. Still bewildered, I penned the following article:

MY LETTER TO THE EDITOR: POST AND COURIER:

"I'd like to tell you about my day as a volunteer at the Patriots Point Maritime and Naval Museum, and why it related to the importance of having the National Medal of Honor Museum here.

"It was Thursday, 25 January 2017. I got to work around 0830, went aboard *Yorktown*, signed in, and had a brief conversation with two of our Veteran volunteers in the volunteer lounge. Then, headed toward The Vietnam Experience, a recreated fire support base typically found all over South Vietnam during the Vietnam War, for my three-hour tour of duty. As I approached the security gate, at about 0850, I noticed two male visitors walking toward the Quonset type building, the entrance to The Vietnam Experience, and enter the door. As I followed, two of our maintenance workers exited the building, pointed toward the door and said, 'Looks like you already have a couple of guest.' I nodded a greeting, and replied, 'Good! Perfect start of my day.'

"Entering the Quonset building, I noticed the two men, who ranged in the age group of the sixties or seventies, eyeballing the information on the wall. I approached with a cherry 'Good Morning. Welcome to our Vietnam.' We shook hands and introduced ourselves. That's how I met Bob and Chuck.

"I quickly discovered one of them had been here before, but a long time ago, and the other man was here for the first time. We continued brief casual conversations, as I began to get into my 'spill' to determine the level of interest and/or involvement they both had on the subject of Vietnam and the war. 'So, you are both veterans of Vietnam,' I casually stated, not knowing what an understatement that remark would become. They each replied in the affirmative. Only half joking I stated, 'You guys may be more knowledgeable than me. Sometimes I learn more than I convey to many of the Vietnam Veterans visiting here.' Then, I made the casual slide into inquiring about when, where, unit, etc., and as my jaw continued yapping in casual conversational tones, one of the men, Bob, reached into his pocket, removed a small pouch, unzipped it, and holding it with both hands, displayed the Medal of Honor (MOH).

"'Wow! A double welcome! Both of you are recipients?' I asked. Both nodded in agreement as Chuck removed his Medal and displayed it to me. Just goes to show that you never know who you might meet at any given time or place as a volunteer at Patriots Point.

"Knowing that I would later look up both of their citations, I avoided delving into those events. As we walked through The Vietnam Experience of our Museum, we continued to exchange anecdotes, tales, yarns, Marine-Army jokes, sea stories and real-life actual experiences through gestures, facial expressions, and conversation relative to each of us being In-Country (Vietnam) during the periods of 1966, 1967, and 1968. It was clear to me that they were enjoying the walk-through of the Vietnam Experience compound. We were briefly together, reliving our individual experiences. These men were articulate, sharp, easy-going, and interesting to be with as they conveyed times of long ago and far away, in unique detail. As an example, while passing one of our numerous displays, one of them pointed out that the upside-down, destroyed jeep in the Khe Sanh area is a M151 A-2 Jeep, which never saw service in Vietnam. Only the M151 A-1 did. That's what I'd call a keen eye for detail.

"Both of these soldiers enjoyed the sounds and sights of *The Vietnam Experience*. We had a pretty thorough tour and exchanged much information. At one time during the walk-through, we were approached by a couple of visitors who were overhearing our conversations and inquired if they could have a photo with the MOH 'winners.' They were quickly and politely corrected to use the term recipient, not winner. They, happily, got their photo and departed excited as a kid in an ice-cream shop.

"Who were these men? Let me tell you about only a brief period of their lives:

"Army Retired Lieutenant Colonel Charles C. 'Chuck' Hagemeister's Medal of Honor citation reads:

For conspicuous gallantry and intrepidity in action at the risk of his life above and beyond the call of duty. While conducting combat operations against a hostile force, Sp5c. Hagemeister's platoon suddenly came under heavy attack from 3 sides by an enemy force occupying well concealed, fortified positions and supported by machine guns and mortars. Seeing 2 of his comrades seriously wounded in the initial action, Sp5c. Hagemeister unhesitatingly and with total disregard for his safety, raced through the deadly hail of enemy fire to provide them medical aid. Upon learning that the platoon leader and several other soldiers also had been wounded, Sp5c. Hagemeister continued to brave the withering enemy fire and crawled forward to render lifesaving treatment and to offer words of encouragement. Attempting to evacuate the seriously wounded soldiers, Sp5c. Hagemeister was taken under fire at close range by an enemy sniper. Realizing that the lives of his fellow soldiers depended on his actions, Sp5c. Hagemeister seized a rifle from a fallen comrade, killed the sniper, 3 other enemy soldiers who were attempting to encircle his position and silenced an enemy machine gun that covered the area with deadly fire. Unable to remove the wounded to a less exposed location and aware of the enemy's efforts to isolate his unit, he dashed through the fusillade of fire to secure help from a nearby platoon. Returning with help, he placed men in positions to cover his advance as he moved to evacuate the wounded forward of his location. These efforts successfully completed, he then moved to the other flank and evacuated additional wounded men despite the fact that his every move drew fire from the enemy. Sp5c. Hagemeister's repeated heroic and selfless actions at the risk of his life saved the lives of many of his comrades and inspired their actions in repelling the enemy assault. Sp5c. Hagemeister's indomitable courage was in the highest traditions of the US Armed Forces and reflects great credit upon himself and the US Army.

"US Army Command Sergeant Major, retired, Robert M. Patterson's official Medal of Honor citation reads:

For conspicuous gallantry and intrepidity in action at the risk of his life above and beyond the call of duty, Sgt. Patterson (then Sp4c.) distinguished himself while serving as a fire team leader of the 3d Platoon, Troop B, during an assault against a North Vietnamese Army battalion which was entrenched in a heavily fortified position. When the leading squad of the 3d Platoon was pinned down by heavy interlocking automatic weapon and rocket propelled grenade fire from 2 enemy bunkers, Sgt. Patterson and the 2 other members of his assault team moved forward under a hail of enemy fire to destroy the bunkers with grenade and machine gun fire. Observing that his comrades were being fired on from a third enemy bunker covered by enemy gunners in 1-man spider holes, Sgt. Patterson, with complete disregard for his safety and ignoring the warning of his comrades that he was moving into a bunker complex, assaulted and destroyed the position. Although exposed to intensive small arm and grenade fire from the bunkers and their mutually supporting emplacements. Sgt. Patterson continued his assault upon the bunkers which were impeding the advance of his unit. Sgt. Patterson singlehandedly destroyed by rifle and grenade fire 5 enemy bunkers, killed 8 enemy soldiers and captured 7 weapons. His dauntless courage and heroism inspired his platoon to resume the attack and to penetrate the enemy defensive position. Sgt. Patterson's action at the risk of his life has reflected great credit upon himself, his unit, and the U.S. Army.

"These are indicative of the type of military men (and perhaps women) the Museum would enshrine. There are only around eighty of these MOH recipients alive today. One of them was a guest speaker at one of my Marine Corps Birthday functions for the Marine Corps Mess of Greenville, and the endorser of my book *A Marine Called Gabe*, James E. Livingston, a Marine Major General, retired, living in Mt Pleasant. All those recipients of the MOH, living and dead, gave so much of themselves at a particular point in their lives, far above the traditional call of duty. They and we deserve a National Museum. And, they and we will eventually get it. Somewhere! It is so utterly unfortunate that the government of Mount Pleasant, SC [**at that time**] did not see the honor and wisdom of establishing a building as a living memorial to all the Medal of Honor recipients because of some self-generated rule that limits height of buildings, or some other unknown reason. By all logical reasons the National Medal of Honor Museum should tower over the landscape, and Patriots Point is the appropriate landscape. Get reasonable folks. Ever hear of a variance? Do you not want the additional income generated by additional visitors? Do you not want the national recognition of being the location of the National Medal of Honor Museum? I'll bet there are other communities who would grab it up in a heartbeat. Your Planning Commission members unanimously made a bad decision. Hopefully, it can be corrected before this rejection proliferates, takes tragic root, and another community may have the honor as the location of the National Medal of Honor Museum. Do any of you not realize that it is not what the museum contains; but rather what the museum embodies that establishes its legacy?

"Major Ralph Stoney Bates, Sr., USMC (Ret)

Mt Pleasant resident"

I continued to believe the rejection could be "worked out." I didn't want to have my city of Mt Pleasant to be the city that rejected the construction of the National Medal of Honor Museum.

The other more memorable and/or unusual incident here at Patriots Point occurred by doing a favor for a friend, another volunteer, Dave Sowers. He called me to state that an old time Marine (he didn't realize I was one of 'em too) by the name of Dave Solberg was a Marine Detachment member on *Yorktown* in the era of 1957-58 and that his daughter was bringing him from Iowa to Patriots Point so he could tour his old duty areas aboard *Yorktown*. Not unusual, it happens many times a year, but this was my first time to escort one of these "old timers" on *Yorktown*. Dave couldn't meet him right away due to another commitment, so I agreed to handle it, and Dave would meet us at about 1100. I talked by telephone to his daughter, Barbara, and we agreed to meet at 0900 on 10 November 2017 at the information desk on the carrier. Interestingly, it was Marine Corps Birthday.

Having never been through the Marine compartments of *Yorktown*, I took a few hours the day before and walked through tour 5 and 6 to familiarize myself with the layout. Fueled with my recon, I met the Solberg's at the appointed time. Now, there were four of them.

The tour went pretty much uneventful, with Marine Solberg initially not recognizing anything, to the point of me wondering if perhaps he was on another carrier. But, finally, he began to see parts of the ship that sharpened his recollection, and soon, we were in the situation where he was conducting the tour for me. That does happen and gets repeated often by visiting veterans of *Yorktown, Laffey*, and *The Vietnam Experience*. Everything was going as expected, that is, until we got to the brig.

In the area of the brig, always manned by Marines in those days, he related a bizarre incident that was so unusual I actually asked him to repeat it for me. Seems they had a standard operating procedure (SOP) drilled into the psyche of those Marines standing that particular watch in that particular place that, under certain conditions, such as total blackout, the armed Marine sentry was to dog the hatch locking himself into that specific compartment, draw his weapon, a military issued .45 Colt automatic, chamber a round, and place the weapon on safe. Then, during the total blackout or whatever other emergency situation dictated by their SOP, if anyone, anyone at all, entered that particular compartment they were to fire upon that person. No warning, no, "halt, who goes there!" Just point and shoot.

Dave Solberg found himself in that compartment when all lights went out and no emergency lighting responded. He dogged the hatch, drew his pistol, and chambered a round. He fumbled with the safety until it clicked on safe, and waited in the darkness. "You could not see anything," he said to me. "It was complete darkness," he added.

After what seemed like an eternity, he heard a hatch un-dog, then close. After a few seconds, he heard soft footsteps slowly coming his way. He took the safety off and waited nervously as the footsteps grew louder and closer. Soon whoever it was, was almost right next to him.

He knew he was supposed to fire, that's what had been drilled into him; however, something compelled him not to. He quickly ensured the safety to be back on, and, gripping tightly, he swung the pistol as hard and fast as he could at whatever or whoever was right there in front of him. His pistol almost jarred from his grip as he connected with whatever or whoever it was, and something or someone hit the deck with a thud. For a few seconds he just froze, breathing heavily. Then, almost as if on cue, all lights came back on, and lying on the deck was the captain of this ship, coldcocked by a Marine sentry who, by-the-way, was supposed to have shot him.

"Unbelievable!" I remarked. "What happened to you?"

"After they took the captain to sick bay, I got my ass chewed like "big-time" by the Gunny for violating my orders and a "thank you" mast from the captain the next day," he responded. "I suppose for not shooting him," he added.

What a story! Never know who you'll run into, or what stories you may hear at Patriots Point.

The stories that fill these pages by me and other volunteers are true events in the lives of many Patriots Point volunteers. They are part of America's treasured assets. On a day-to-day basis, individually and collectively, these men and women Volunteers of Patriots Point listen, learn, convey, and establish their own addition to the legacy of the Americans of World War II, Korea, and Vietnam Wars telling, explaining and honoring all those men, and women also, who continue to walk in the footsteps of heroes, today, yesterday, and tomorrow. They are Patriots Point Volunteers.

CHAPTER 12
VOLUNTEER JOANNE HANN

★★★

JoAnne Hann: Photo property of author

Growing up in a large traditional second-generation Italian family, with four Joes, three Josephine's and a large assortment of colorful Italian characters made for an intense lifestyle for this introvert—that was me, back in my younger days. The family was tightly knit with my grandfather at the head. He had a green grocery business at the famous

Lexington Market in Baltimore and did so well that he and my grandmother, Nanni, had a home in the city and a second shore home on the Magothy River off the Chesapeake Bay. We would go down and spend weekends there in the summer and I remember in the evenings, after a wonderful Italian meal, we would sing Italian songs on the porch. My dad would play the guitar and my uncle would play the mandolin. Everyone would drink wine and my colorful Aunt Marie and Uncle Vince would often get a little tipsy. I remember when that happened, you could expect Uncle Vince's pants to fall down at some point while he stood there singing in his boxers. We all laughed and laughed, even though we had seen that act many times before. I am also very proud that my three uncles who have since passed were all awarded the Combat Infantry Badge, two in France and one in Italy during WWII and my husband, Joe, is an Army veteran who served in the First Battalion of the Third Infantry (the Old Guard) at Ft. Myer, Virginia.

As the eldest of five, and after attending a staunch, traditional Catholic Elementary School and Andover High School, it resulted in me realizing I had to develop a skill that would give me a marketable trade so I could escape the noisy bundled household, and live on my own, by my own standards. Always a good student, fast to learn, and eager to acquire new skills, I found the attribute of stenography very interesting and excelled in that venue. If you were to ask me why stenography, I'm not sure exactly why. It just was that I found I could do it almost naturally, while it was always challenging to keep up with the speaker while keeping your notes legible. And, it proved the best choice for me.

The FBI, yes, that FBI, was conducting interviews at my high school around the same time I won the school's top awards for typing and stenography. I wanted, and needed a job after high school and the Federal Bureau of Investigation filled that void. Having a guaranteed job after graduation was ideal, so off to work I went to Washington, D.C. at the Washington Field Office of the Federal Bureau of Investigation. I remember thinking, "What a great beginning of developing a resume."

Resumes first line: *Worked for the FBI in the Washington Field Office*! Wow! This will look terrific on my continuing-to-be-developed job resume.

Working at the Bureau was great and I was assigned to take all kinds of verbal field reports directly from Agents either at the office or over the phone. Trust me. You learn a lot of new words doing a thing like that. Being so young, politics was the last thing on my mind. Other than debating the Vietnam War with "Flower Child" types, even with my "America, love it or leave it" attitude, I was pretty much apolitical—the perfect stenographer, in the perfect job.

I transcribed dictated reports on Daniel Ellsberg (The Pentagon Papers), the Watergate break-in, the Black Panthers , the Weatherman, or Weather Underground, and the Students for a Democratic Society (SDS). I had great faith in the church and in our great country and not much tolerance for those against traditional, fundamental beliefs. So, my work made me feel like I was providing a great service in helping the Bureau capture many radicals and criminals. I felt really good about doing the task assigned to me. I felt a part of something good.

In my second year at the Bureau, I enjoyed working mostly with agents on the bank robbery squad. I remember the first time I heard about the red-dye bundles hidden inside money bags, that would usually explode in the robber's getaway cars, and how ingenious I thought that was.

I left the FBI to join the Rouse Company, a very large developing firm that had lots of money from its leasing of shopping malls all over the country. It was a company founded by James W. Rouse and Hunter Moss in 1939, and became a publicly held company in 1956, until 2004 when General Growth Company purchased it. The great benefit I received many times over was a week of vacations in one of their vacation rental properties that were reserved for company employees at no charge. Often, I took my noisy Italian family with me so my mom and dad could get away and relax. They did so much for me growing up, and it was a good way to share my good fortune with them, and I actually enjoyed these times with my Italian Mom and Dad a great deal.

Not only did The Rouse Company provide their employees with wonderful benefits, it was also a very progressive organization, and a place of great growth opportunity. While employed there, the company purchased a mini-computer to eventually replace the large IBM main-frame, and I was asked if I wanted to learn how to operate the mini-computer. Loving a challenge, I accepted the new position and eventually became a computer programmer, a Local Area Network Manager, and then, a new title: Information Technology Manager, for various companies. I have always been the type of person that enjoys the challenge of continuous improvement. I've never simply sat and vegetated in some rote memory job anywhere or anytime. I have this desire to continuously improve, so over time, while working full time and while raising our son, I earned a B.S. Degree in Business with an emphasis on Computers from the College of Notre Dame of Maryland and a M.S. Degree in Information Technology from Johns Hopkins University. Taking courses was fun because it gave my husband, Joe and I, lots to discuss.

Back then, very few women were in the technology field so I was a pioneer in a sense. For instance, I would go to conferences and training sessions that were attended by mostly men using lots of techie acronyms. I felt lucky if one or two other women were there. It was just the way it was in those days. Interestingly, technical people usually brought the latest, coolest devices to these events and keyboarded away with eye contact kept to a minimum. If you brought pen and paper you were considered a "dinosaur." Even today, a techie is referred to as the "computer guy" and people mostly expect a male to fix their computer. However, fixing computers was my least favorite thing to do. I liked managing corporate applications, servers, and networks. I remember when I was first promoted to a management position for a telecommunications manufacturing and distribution company that employed about 200 people. I was one of two computer programmers, the other, being a guy who was constantly finding fault in my work and pointing it out to my boss. I figured I must have been a real threat to him. However, when the company downsized, he was let go but I kept my job. I had access to payroll so I knew it was not because he was making a higher salary than me. To this day I am not sure why it was him and not me but I was grateful that my boss had continued faith in my abilities and knew that people tend to like me. Moreover, when the boss took another position, I was promoted to his and moved into a nice window office. Not bad and I stayed on with this company for eight years before joining Johns Hopkins University.

After working for fifteen years at Hopkins as an IT Manager/Systems Engineer, Joe and I retired and moved to Mount Pleasant, SC. Having been born and raised in Baltimore, moving south to a warmer climate was appealing. So in 2011, we looked around in Florida since we have family there, but it did not feel quite right. We had visited Charleston on our honeymoon a long time ago and planned to check out the area. So how did we end up in Mount Pleasant? Well, I went to have my teeth cleaned. My usual hygienist was out so a substitute filled in for her. We got to talking about retirement locations, and she exclaimed that she had heard Mount Pleasant was a wonderful place to live. I remember feeling this was a divine intervention, so two weeks later we came and fell in love with the area. A couple of months later, we bought our house and decided it would be a good rental, so while we continued to work our jobs in Maryland, we rented the house to a man who worked for Boeing. Boeing had recently opened a new non-union plant near Charleston International Airport. Once we retired, we sold the house in Maryland and moved here, initially living in a rental on the beach for four months while our house in Mount Pleasant was renovated. This proved to be very healing and helped us de-stress from the transition.

Fortunately, as a retiree, my life has been greatly simplified. I swore as I approached retirement I would only do those things I love, like Zumba dancing, cooking, yoga, pickle ball, and driving the Shuttle bus at Patriots Point. Believe it or not, driving the shuttle is a challenge. To any doubters, try it on a crowded day with hundreds of little ones running around, or attempting to maneuver the "Blue Whale," as some call the enclosed shuttle, around crowded causeways and docks containing those who have no idea what—WALKING LANE and DRIVING LANE means. But, even then, even with that, it's enjoyable. You get to meet interesting people from virtually everywhere. I especially enjoy the military veterans, both the visitors and those working and volunteering here at the Naval and Maritime Museum. This is a fun job.

CHAPTER 13
VOLUNTEER ROBERT NEWMAN

★★★

Robert Newman: Photo property of author

As a junior officer in the US Navy, I learned many of life's lessons:

I was a twenty-three-year-old Ensign, Engineering Duty Officer (EDO) on the USS *Albany* CG-10 in 1970. Everyone in the Navy knows that an Ensign is about the lowest form of life on the ship especially as a "Snipe" (Engineering Propulsion). Everyone also knows when you are relieved from watch, you must go through in unique detail, the status of the propulsion plant in a conversation with your watch relief. To not do this is a very big infraction of the rules. In short, it ain't the Navy way. It usually takes about five minutes to go through the status of the propulsion plant:

Such as which boilers are on the line, which feed pumps are running, which fire pumps are running, etc., etc.

My ship had been steaming in the Mediterranean for ten days at a steady 10 knots. That can put any sailor asleep at the wheel. We had not had a speed change at any time in in those ten days. Everyone aboard that vessel was bored, cranky, and tired. I had the mid-watch (12:00 AM to 4:00 AM) as the Engineer-In-Charge of Propulsion Central Control. When my watch relief finally arrived ten minutes late, it upset me to no ends. As my anger had been rising to a boiling point, when he finally made his appearance, very belatedly, I was very angry and loudly blurted out to him—***You are late! Nothing has changed! I am going to bed!***

As I turned around to leave Central Control, I was shocked, then—stunned, to see that the Chief Engineer was not in his stateroom asleep, as I assumed he was; instead, he was standing right behind me during my out-burst toward my relief. He was, fully dressed, wearing, not only his uniform, but an annoyed facial expression that caused me to know something was coming at me that I would not like. I had not properly reviewed the status with my watch relief. I was up the preverbal creek without a paddle. I will not even try to express in writing what he said to me, and how he expressed those words. It's still painful to this day. Some of the words are not found in the English Dictionary, and some of the words I had never heard before. I didn't even know they existed. Needless to say, it was the worst cursing-out (swearing) I have ever heard, before or since. I have never forgotten, nor will I ever forget.

However, as painful as it was at the time, and it was a painful, brutally short, and a very meaningful learning experience, it helped me in my career in the Navy, and even in the after-the-Navy life. It was a life-altering moment that lasted a lifetime.

Regressing a bit, there is another interesting story: When I arrived onboard my ship as a brand new Ensign, deployed to the Sixth Fleet, I received a message that I was assigned the collateral duty as the Jewish Lay Leader for the ship. I immediately went to the Chaplin, who was a full Commander, and explained that I was not very religious, and I did not want this assignment. Perhaps I was just uneasy about that type of assigned duty, or perhaps I simply felt that I wasn't qualified. I'm not sure. His response was blunt and direct. "Are you an officer?" He stood directly in front of me and stared directly into my eyes. My reply was "Yes, I am an Ensign." Then, still glaring, he asked, "Do you have ***Jewish*** on your dog tags." I responded, "Yes sir." Then, the Chaplin spoke very sternly, still looking right into my eyes, "Then you are the Jewish Lay Leader." As I unwisely started to open my mouth, he finished, "No more discussion!" That was that. Wisely, I did not open or even attempt to open my mouth.

As I was leaving his stateroom, he called out to me, "Ensign, there is a big benefit to being the Jewish Lay Leader, and that is you get to keep the only officially permitted alcoholic beverage on the ship! I turned toward him as he approached. With a smiling face, he handed me a bottle of Navy issued Mogen David wine, and finished with this verbal warning, "Use this for religious purposes only!"

After our first service, the word got out that the Jewish Sailors were drinking wine during their religious service, and that attracted a few more sailors to participate. I won't say they were converts; however, a taste of wine can bring attendance at a religious service on a Navy ship higher than the average.

As a Yorktown Volunteer:

I was at the Information Desk aboard *Yorktown*, when a man, well into his 80s, walked up and asked me how to get to the escalator. I told him where it is located, but his question puzzled me. So I asked him why he wanted to see the escalator. His response was, ***I was an Electrician's Mate on this ship for four years in the 1960s, and about all I did was work on the damn escalator. As much as I worked on it, it never did work very well.*** My response back to him was, ***Please check it out again. It is still not running right!***

★★★

Here is another true story, and maybe you can enhance with a little more humor:

This is one of the most interesting questions I have had at the Yorktown Information Desk:

A man and woman with two children came up to the Information Desk while I was on-duty. In response to several of their queries, I gave them the general download about five of the self-guided tours, Tour 3 Flight Deck, bathrooms at bow and stern, and how CV 10 got its name *Yorktown* were covered. They were very interested, and after my briefing, the woman and children walked away, but the man lingered around the Information Desk.

After a minute or two, the man gestured for me to lean over the desk because he wanted to whisper something to me. His whispered comment was, "I am going to propose marriage to that lady on board *Yorktown* today!" Then he added, "Where would be the right place on USS *Yorktown* for me to propose?"

Since there is nothing in our Volunteer Training, in the Volunteer Manual, or in the Butt Card on this subject, I had to think fast. First, I thought about the Chapel on Tour 1, but then I realized that would not be outside, and outside was better because it was a nice day. Then I thought about the Flight Deck, but there would be too many people there looking around, so I told him the best place would be the on the fantail at the stern looking out at Charleston Harbor. Then I added, "Let me know what she says."

He never came back to talk to me during my shift, but I did see him walk by with a big smile on his face, so I think I know the answer. I wonder if he was the first to propose to a potential bride in the seventy-five year history of USS *Yorktown* CV-10 while actually on the ship.

NOTE:ROBERT,WHATWASYOURAFTER-THE-NAVY-LIFE?

My career after the Navy was thirty-four years with a company manufacturing railroad track construction and maintenance machinery. Started as Design Mechanical Engineer and my last twenty-one years, was, as the President of the company. I am married with two children and three grandchildren.

CHAPTER 14
VOLUNTEER DAVE SOWERS

★★★

Dave Sowers: Photo property of author

A RECRUIT'S DAY ONE

The bus turned south and the bright lights of the Charleston airport faded into a darkened landscape, and the scene became sparsely populated and illuminated only by a few twinkling lights here and there. It was almost ten pm as I sat staring out the window, tired but alert, my thoughts drifting back to how I came to be here in the first place . . .

My decision to join the Marine Corps was driven by four factors and culminated in the second semester of my senior year in high school.

First, came the realization that me going to college was, to put it mildly, a huge stretch, a target that was way beyond range. In short, in all probability, it simply wasn't going to happen. Oh, I wasn't a bad student. I just wasn't a good student. Some would say that I was somewhat lacking in educational motivation. Or, as my high school counselor had defined me—***lazy***. That was a scientific definition on her part that pretty much hit the nail on the head. Hell, I'd been in school for twelve years, what else was there to learn. No, I was done with that kind of education and ready to meet the big wide world head-on. Or, so I thought.

This brings me to the second factor. I wanted to travel and see the world. I had been raised in a small town in southwest Virginia. Not a *one-stoplight place*, but not too far from it, at the same time. You could call it Mayberry's (of Mayberry RFD) slightly larger sister, maybe. I'd heard of "the world," seen it on TV, but at almost eighteen-years-old, still hadn't experienced this thing called travel. Yes, I wanted to see the "world," travel to far-away places, and experience grown-up stuff in a grown-up place far from home.

Thirdly, I was indeed patriotic, believing that it was the duty of every male, eighteen or older, to do his duty and serve his country. To give back some measure of what had been provided to him, like security, protection, and the freedom to live life untroubled by hostile nations. It was the young male's responsibility to defend and protect those who needed that protection. This was my thought process. And, in those days, many other young males agreed. It's just the way it was.

And finally, being the son of a World War II Marine, who had served proudly and honorably, had a lot to do with it. My father was a veteran of four island invasions in the south Pacific, and I had grown up in the shadow of this proud Marine. Although he didn't talk much about his experiences, I knew he had been tested in battle and was deeply moved by it all. I saw his 24th Marine Regiment plaque, his dress blues with medals, all packed away in a trunk, his Purple Heart Medal, his photos from places like Camp Lejeune, California, and Hawaii and his souvenirs from Saipan, Tinian, Roi-Namur, and Iwo Jima. He carried a "souvenir" in his neck from Iwo, courtesy of a Japanese mortar round on the beach that sent him to a naval hospital and also ended his time in the Corps.

All that added up to a decision that made perfect sense to me. My mother cried when I told her, my dad was pleased, to say the least. The traveling Marine recruiter was contacted, and an appointment set up, followed by interviews, a short aptitude test, and a date set for a physical exam. Since I was seventeen and still in high school, I would have to be sworn in as a Marine Reservist and then, after graduating high school, sworn into the regular Marine Corps.

It was a quickly arranged bus ride to Beckley, West Virginia for my physical, then further on to Charleston, West Virginia, where I spent the night in the Marine Reserve barracks before being sworn-in by a lieutenant the next morning. There were handshakes and backslapping all around, then, suddenly, off to the bus station for my return trip home.

I'm a Marine kept running through my head; however, I had no idea what I would have to do to actually <u>earn</u> that title.

Eleven weeks later, June 30, 1964, after memorizing my serial number and the ten General Orders of a Marine Guard, I made the trip in reverse and was sworn-in, along with three others, into the regular

Marine Corps. Oddly, I thought, there were no handshakes or back-slaps this time, only an order to "police-up" the squad-bay.

Afterwards, I was pulled aside by the lieutenant and handed four large envelopes which contained our orders. I was put in charge of the four of us and told it was my responsibility to get us to Parris Island. I was also told (actually warned would be a better word), that one of our group was considered a possible *runner,* having been "encouraged" to join the Marine Corps by a local judge, whose daughter was in a family way, apparently caused by our travelling companion. We could sense he was beginning to have second thoughts about the whole thing. He was a big boy, probably half again my size and weight and I knew right then that, if he chose to run, the best I had to offer wouldn't stop him. I made sure he got wedged in between us on the trip to the airport and had a window seat on our first flight. Thankfully, he didn't put up any overt resistance.

My first flight ever was from Charleston to Bluefield, West Virginia in a Piedmont DC-3. Most spectacular! Then, we flew on to Roanoke, Virginia, where we had a short layover before catching another DC-3 for our flight to Winston-Salem, North Carolina.

During our layover in Roanoke, I noticed a Marine sergeant in an adjacent waiting area. Approaching him in conversation, I saw him chuckle when he saw the orders I was carrying, and we struck up a short, but meaningful conversation. I asked him what Parris Island was like, and what to expect in boot camp. His answer was short, sweet, and sobering, "Life as you know it is over," he said with a cunning smile. "You're going to think the world has **&#*%* (expletives deleted) ended." I thought, wow! This was a most disturbing and direct description of what we were facing, and quite at odds from what the recruiter had referred to as an excellent opportunity to get in great physical shape while learning the basics of being (not becoming, but BEING) a Marine. I wisely chose not to share this with my fellow travelers, especially the father-to-be.

After an uneventful flight to Winston-Salem, we changed planes again, this time a jet, for the trip to Charleston, South Carolina. The Sergeant's warnings were beginning to fade as my first jet flight captured my attention and imagination.

Deplaning in Charleston, we were directed to a waiting area marked PARRIS ISLAND. It was explained to us by an airport employee that we were to wait in that location until others destined for Parris Island had arrived. We were to be waiting until a full bus load was present before departure. We would know this because, at the proper time, a bus would appear just outside and the driver would invite us aboard the bus for the trip to Parris Island.

"Splendid," I thought to myself, *"they have this all thought out. A bus! We'll board a bus for a leisurely trip to the Island. Being late, they'll probably show us to our sleeping accommodations, bid us good night, and wake us in time for breakfast the following day. Maybe even take our food orders that night to save time in the morning. Splendid, indeed! That Sergeant obviously was trying to play some huge joke on me. Possibly he was just trying to scare me. Well, he didn't mention the bus, so what did he know? Maybe that was the way it was in the 'Old Corps' but we were a new generation, we couldn't be expected to suffer the slings and arrows he alluded to. No, life as we know it would continue in the civilized manner to which we had become accustomed."* Of this I was sure!

I shared these thoughts with my fellow travelers as a few others joined us in the waiting area. Young men arrived from New York, Philadelphia, Baltimore, and Cleveland. We had a grand time, joking, smoking, and telling tall tales about all that we had accomplished in our short lives. We told lies about the girls we had dated and deluded ourselves with speculation of what things lie ahead. Several had heard horror stories but, since none of us had experienced it, we collectively blew it all off as hearsay.

Before long the waiting area was full and soon after that the bus arrived outside. As we all stood to leave, a janitor's voice mocked out, "you'll be sooorrry," which brought nervous laughter from the group. Sorry? Hah!

The bus was spacious, clean, and modern and we filed on to take our seats. The driver was polite, not saying much, but polite and it seemed to me that everyone was probably like that in South Carolina and Parris Island was going to be a real swell place. Someone had mentioned swimming so I assumed the place had a pool. Wow, a pool! This stuff was sounding better by the minute.

As I sat there, gazing at the lights of the airport, it dawned on me that today was, indeed, a highpoint in my short life. I had traveled from home to Charleston, West Virginia all by myself for the second time. I had been sworn into the Marine Corps. I had flown in an airplane for the first, second, third, and fourth times in my life, all in one day. And now I was in South Carolina, another first, with a fine bunch of lads it seemed, off on a great adventure. This was my day!

I don't know how long the bus ride took but the blackness of the night made it seem like forever. We were still talking, and laughing, and smoking as we approached the Main Gate Guard Post. The bus stopped, doors opened, and a tall MP in uniform boarded, turned to face us, and bellowed ***PUT 'EM OUT***, which we quickly did. It was obvious from his tone that this was not a request. He then turned away from us and stood at parade rest as the driver closed the doors and drove across the causeway to the island. You could hear a pin drop. Apart from the sound of the bus engine nothing could be heard. By some measure of self-preservation we had, as a group, deduced that silence was the best foot to put forward here.

After a short ride - *in silence* - we arrived at what we would later learn was Recruit Receiving Barracks. The bus stopped, door opened, and the MP departed.

And the world, as we knew it, ended!

From my position near the center of the bus, I didn't quite see the two Marine Drill Instructors (DI's) come aboard, but I sure heard them.

GET THE (expletive deleted) ***OFF MY*** (expletive deleted) ***BUS, RIGHT*** (expletive deleted) ***NOW! MOVE, MOVE, MOVE!*** I must admit, in hindsight, that I didn't realize it was **HIS** bus. If I had, I'm not sure I would have gotten on it in the first place. There was no time for thought, or anything else for that matter. We were moving, moving, moving, and as I leapt to my feet, I was carried along down the aisle as we desperately sought to be outside, away from these mad-men.

But it wasn't to be! Outside was no haven as another DI was throwing perhaps the biggest hissy fit I had ever seen, imploring us to ***LINE UP, STAND AT ATTENTION, EYES FRONT, DON'T YOU*** (expletive deleted) ***LOOK AT ME***. I don't remember the yellow footprints, but I must have stood on them in an acceptable manner because the only admonishment I received from him was not to (expletive deleted) look at him. As he was standing squarely in front of me, I wanted to tell him that I wasn't trying to (expletive deleted) look at him but his position made that (expletive deleted) impossible. One thing that has allowed me to live as long as I have is my ability to read people by their body language. He didn't seem to be the kind that takes criticism, constructive or otherwise, in the manner it may be presented. Or any other manner to be honest, so, I exercised extreme caution and remained silent. Which was a serious mistake since he had just asked me; ***DO YOU*** (expletive deleted) ***UNDERSTAND ME?*** This whole thing was going downhill exponentially with my *pucker-factor* going in the opposite direction just as fast! You could not have driven a ten penny nail up my rear-end with a ten pound sledgehammer.

Yes sir, I stammered, not entirely sure what to say. Apparently he had hearing problems because even though he was standing in front of me, his face now dangerously close to mine, he roared ***I CAN'T HEAR YOU!!*** I literally roared back, ***SIR, YES, SIR!!*** He glared at me, ***I CAN'T HEAR YOU!!!***, came his response, several tens of decibels higher. We obviously had a communication problem here, and I was seriously concerned that this could go on indefinitely, so I screwed up every ounce of diaphragm pressure I had and bellowed, at the top of my lungs ***SIR, YES SIR!!*** That seemed to satisfy him somewhat, and he moved on to some other hapless lad behind me.

By now the bus was empty, and we had three extremely agitated DI's appearing to be everywhere at once, asking strange questions for which there were no polite answers. ***Sir, yes sir, sir, no sir, sir, no excuse sir!*** We learned quickly. You do in situations like that, or you simply don't last. We learned to pick things up when told, we learned to move forward when told, we learned when to stop moving when told, we learned to put things down when told, and some of us learned our right from our left. All, in a matter of a few extremely frightening moments. It was apparently enough of the basics to get us into the Receiving Barracks and seated. Collectively we were *ladies*, individually we were *maggots.* These *gentle* terms of *endearment* would become indelibly ingrained in our minds, bodies, and spirits until the day we graduated this boot camp.

At some point during this *welcoming,* it occurred to me that I might have made a judgmental error in my strategy to see the "world." But these three DIs didn't seem to be taking confessions, so I kept it to myself.

My first day in the Marine Corps was coming to an end. We would be shown to our sleeping accommodations, but it wouldn't be for several more grueling hours before that happened, and we would be rudely roused from sleep long before the sun came up. No menu for breakfast was provided to us.

Then, the transformation began. Over the course of the next twelve-weeks things became clearer. We learned. We became conditioned. We adapted. We overcame. We grew toward becoming a Marine. Gradually! Then, one day, it happened. We became Marines.

But, that's entirely another story.

Semper Fi.

CHAPTER 15

VOLUNTEER LISA ISAACSON

★★★

I sent an email to several of our volunteers, asking if they would agree to a story for the anthology *Short Rations From Patriots Point Volunteers.* One of the replies is as follows:

Stoney,

As I have no military experience in my background, I don't feel I could do your book justice.

I'm just a retired teacher (who was not born in this country) who really enjoys meeting people and finding out a little bit about them, such as where they come from, and what brought them to Patriots Point Naval and Maritime Museum. Being trilingual, I have had the opportunity to speak to many foreigners in their language, and in many cases I have helped them out in different ways, such as where to find good food, what places to visit, and other things a foreigner might need while visiting here.

That's all I got- not even a full page!

Good luck with your book and hope you get more responses.

Lisa Isaacson

Shuttle driver

As a result of her response, I found Lisa very unique. My response to her was as follows:

Oh the contrary, Lisa. Yours is a most interesting story and adds to the diversity of our volunteers here at Patriots Point.

Please respond to the following questions and statements:

This is her story:

Tell me a bit about yourself:

I am Lisa Isaacson, and I was born in the Dominican Republic and came to the United States with my parents when I was five-years-old. I grew up in Rochester, NY and attended school at Brockport State College of New York, and graduated from that school with degrees in Spanish and German. After graduation, I continued my education and gained a Master's Degree in English as a Second Language (ESL), which has enabled me to be a very proud teacher for thirty-five years; thus, it has allowed me to converse with a wide range of visitors here at Patriots Point and likewise during my years while I was working in my teaching career. My last teaching assignment was at Edgewood City School District in South Western Ohio. Now, I am, very proudly, a retired teacher.

Working in education is, in a way, similar to being in the military, as far as moving around is concerned. First, my husband went to Berkeley for a PhD in Chemistry. We had married (in Rochester) and moved to California right away. Then there were several post-graduate positions as he waited for a good tenure-track position to come along. After Berkeley, he did two years at Brookhaven Labs on Long Island. The first year there I got my Masters (ESL) at Stony Brook. The second year I taught at a nearby high school. Then off for a year to Minneapolis, where he did another post-doc at the University of Minnesota. There I taught English as a Second Language (ESL) to adult Indochinese refugees. They actually had a state-funded program for all-day instruction for these adults. From there we ended up at Oxford, Ohio for 30 years. My husband was a Chemistry professor at Miami University. Miami of Ohio, that is.

Lisa, tell a little bit about you growing up:

I came to this country at the age of five, not knowing one word of English. I was thrown into the first grade and struggled. Obviously it was a shock to the system of a little foreign child who could speak only German and Spanish. But with the help of teachers and neighbors, and by being very young, I was able to learn English very quickly. Back then, there were not many immigrants and we didn't have the option of seeing signs, pamphlets, etc. in languages other than English. I was fortunate to be able to travel every summer back to the Dominican Republic to be with my German grandmother and aunt and uncle.

Later, my relatives moved to the States (yes, they took me along) when the political situation in the Dominican Republic was getting too dangerous for them. As I grew up speaking German and Spanish, while in college, I spent a semester in Germany as a student-teacher.

What compelled you to go into the teaching profession?

I looked at teaching as a calling. You've got to love kids and your subject matter enough to work for low pay, with little respect from the community and very challenging conditions. As long as I can remember, I've wanted to be a teacher. Don't know why, except that I really feel it's a calling.

Any particular teaching experience that is most memorable to you?

In general, due to my husband's career, we moved often; therefore, I had the opportunity to teach in numerous environments. I am very grateful for that experience. But, to respond specifically to your question, the fifteen trips with student groups to Europe would have to be the highlight of my teaching experience. For example, once, after much cajoling and encouragement, I had a student, utilizing her learned German language, purchase a souvenir in a local shop in Germany. She entered the shop alone, made her purchase, and came out smiling ear-to-ear and blustered out to me: "It works! It really works!"

It was numerous things like that which continues validating to me that what I was doing was definitely worthwhile.

Thanks to social media, I keep in contact with many of my former students. There is nothing more rewarding than to receive a note, as I did, from a former student who was a trouble-maker then, who is now a teacher himself, apologizing for his "terrible behavior" when he was in my class. Then, just as I am writing this, that part about taking students to Europe and practicing what they learned in the classroom being the best part? Well—recently I reconnected with a former student who is in charge of the Information Technology (IT) Department for King Estate Wineries in Oregon, and I just received a case of wine this morning from him!!! Now, how does THAT get any better? HA!

Doesn't get any better.

What brought you to the Charleston area?

Simple, all the boxes on our bucket-list were checked off.

And, what caused you to volunteer at Patriots Point?

I wanted to volunteer somewhere meaningful, and couldn't really find that special place that was exciting for me. That is, until a volunteer from here mentioned Patriots Point to me. The description sounded perfect. It's totally different from anything I've ever done in my life. I've learned so much and am so appreciative of our military veterans, who work and volunteer here, and to those who visit here.

Of the hundreds of visitors you have come in contact with, would you relate the most memorable.

The answer is not a single event, but multiple events. Let me explain. I enjoy the German-speaking ones. I had a couple who were SO happy I spoke to them in their language. They took that opportunity to ask for recommendations for all sorts of things. And, one afternoon I had two Italian men on my shuttle. By the end of the one minute ride, we were chatting and laughing, and on their departure from my shuttle, they kissed me on each cheek! At least I knew enough not to slap them - after all, they were Italian!

Also, I love chatting with the military veterans, especially the ones who have served on *Yorktown*.

The veterans are always the ones who thank ME for volunteering! I find that so ironic. They are so humble. I pretty much find most of the visitors riding on my shuttle, in some way, memorable. When I walk in the door after an afternoon driving the shuttle at Patriots Point, my husband always asks, "So, who did you meet today and what stories do you have for me today?"

If you had anything to do over again, what would it be, and why?

Easy answer. Nothing! I have no regrets in life. I feel blessed, and I feel that everything happens for a reason.

Anything to add?

Yes. It makes me sad at how veterans are mistreated in this country. Not sure how to turn that around. But, it needs turning around. They deserve more.

I drive the shuttle on Mondays, 3 to 6 pm.

CHAPTER 16

VOLUNTEER CHIP BIERNBAUM

★★★

Received the following email from Chip after a successful Patriots Point Volunteer's trip to Washington, DC and Fort Bragg:

To: RALPH BATES <ralynbat@bellsouth.net>
From: Chip Biernbaum <cXXXXXX1@bellsouth.net>
Sent: Sunday, October 7, 2018 3:44 PM
Subject: Re: My Bio draft for your book

Chip in Vietnam. Photo property of author.

Okay, here it is, Stoney:

I was born in New Jersey in December 1946, and grew up in Woodstown, a small town in southern NJ. After graduating from Woodstown High School in 1964, I attended Wake Forest University in Winston-Salem, NC, where I earned a Bachelor of Science in biology. After graduating, I began my graduate work at the University of Connecticut (UConn).

During my first year at UConn in 1969, I was a research assistant on a spring trip to Antarctica to study bottom-dwelling invertebrates in the Weddell Sea, just east of the Antarctic Peninsula. We took off from Quonset Point, Rhode Island, and then traveled to Punta Arenas, Chile (on the Strait of Magellan) via overnight stops in St. Croix, Panama, Lima, and Santiago. Our aircraft was the C-124 Globemaster II (also known as "Old Shakey"), a large plane with a small nose-like button for an anterior radome and a large, expansive, clam-shaped anterior opening. The aircraft was extraordinarily slow — at one point, I looked out the small porthole and a car on the Chilean Pan-American Highway passed us! In Punta Arenas, we picked up our vessel, the 310-foot-long, heavy icebreaker USCGC *Glacier* (WAGB-4), capable of breaking ice up to twenty feet thick (when using the tactic of backing up and ramming the ice) and of continuous breaking of four-foot-thick ice at 3 knots. We did our research for two months in the Weddell Sea, hundreds of miles from land. In addition to having an oceanography research team from Norway aboard, we had a fellow from the University of Washington doing bottom core samples and researchers from Canada studying several species of seals and penguins (their daily day-night physiology was studied because polar animals are not subjected to our twenty-four-hour cycle). Whenever, these animals had to be brought aboard the ship, they would be airlifted by chopper with a sling below. Researchers would leave the vessel, walk across the ten-foot-thick ice, and anesthetize the seals and penguins for transport. On one occasion, I had the opportunity to do that — a strange sensation with the ocean swells lifting the ice below your feet. There was no difficulty in approaching the seals — we look and walk like penguins. Choppers were also used to look for open areas in the ice (polynyas) where we could do our sampling. The scenery was beautiful: dozens of large icebergs having iridescent shades of blue embedded in the ice within view of the ship. When we were in open seas, it would sometimes take us most of a day to pass by some of the larger "tabular" bergs. Our team studied the animals that lived on the sea floor 1,000 to 4,000 meters below us (commonly it took one to three hours for our sampling gear — usually a giant four by eight foot sled or a sampling device similar to a steam-shovel's grab — to reach the bottom). Rather unexpectedly, the bottom was made up largely of masses of sponge spicules (undecomposable silicon dioxide needles embedded in sponge tissue as an anti-predatory mechanism) and foraminiferans (small, calcareous, unicellular organisms ranging in size from a bb to a half-inch, plus our expected crustaceans, mollusks, brittle stars, etc. On one occasion, we were stuck in the ice (there was no larger icebreaker that could rescue us) and they had dynamite charges set (but not used). The thought was that if the ship had to overwinter in the ice, scientific crew and unnecessary ship's company would be evacuated by helicopter and the others remained to overwinter (there was a year's worth of food aboard). Fortunately, we had great food: frog legs, lobster, steak, and, like our British brethren, the "Coasties" had a can of beer each week. Our plane was delayed on its return flight to Punta Arenas by over a week due to a malfunctioning engine, so I spent that period of time eating untoasted *Toast'em Pop Ups* for each meal (the only food I could recognize as being manufactured in the US) to avoid getting Montezuma's Revenge (a colleague had gotten the ailment on a research cruise a year earlier and it lasted for many months.)

After completing my first year at the University of Connecticut, I took a trip to my draft board in New Jersey to see what the odds were that I could be drafted before finishing my graduate studies in three years (my estimate of the time necessary for completion). After the clerk looked it up, she informed me that "I was on the draft list for next month." After that sobering revelation, I took a leave-of-absence from UConn, tried without any success to enlist in the Navy at a stop at the recruiting office in Washington, DC (they wanted a four-year obligation — no surprise in the 1960s!), and then joined the "Green Machine" (US Army), in June of 1969.

On July 21, 1969, I stood in front of the draft board with a group of fellow inductees and waited for a bus to take us to Ft. Dix, NJ, for our basic training. I remember that specific date because that evening Neil Armstrong of Apollo 11 was to step off the Apollo lander to take his first steps on the moon. When we arrived at the new-soldiers barracks, we were told that we were restricted to the building (the Army was afraid that new draftees would have second thoughts and some of them would desert to Canada or elsewhere to avoid Vietnam). However, I knew that Neil Armstrong was going to put his first steps on the moon that evening. I decided that, even if I were caught and they threw the book at me, it was worth doing something to see that first step on the moon. So I snuck out of the new-soldiers barracks and walked down the base road to look for a TV screen. I found one at a large building that had many pay telephones for soldiers to call their families. I sat there and watched as Neil Armstrong took his first steps on the moon, uttering that famous statement: "That's one small step for [a] man, one giant leap for mankind." I then wandered back to the new-soldiers barracks.

After basic training, I was surprised to learn that I was being sent to Military Police (MP) School at Fort Gordon, Georgia. [Stoney, I just missed you — I was there until July of 1970. I think I was in the 4th AIT, but it was on a long circuitous road on the top of a hill, where the barracks were arranged along the road.] Because I was all of 125 pounds soaking wet, I asked of what use I would be as an MP. I was told that if I had trouble with the patrons of a bar (drunk & disorderly, to put it mildly), all the GIs would see was my MP uniform and nothing else. That well-delivered false statement somewhat relieved me. Unfortunately, during training I seriously fractured my ankle during judo training in MP School, so I couldn't graduate on time. Unexpectedly, I had orders to report to Germany after completing MP School. Those orders were ultimately modified. While I was in my two-month "holding pattern," I picked up trash and put it in a dump truck (difficult with a full-leg cast) and served as a test subject for guys (Army, FBI, Secret Service, etc.) who were being trained to be polygraph examiners. They would take about twelve of us from the MP Company and put us two to a room. They would then take the two guys out of a room and have them "do a crime," such as cut a wire at a nearby electrical installation. The two guys would return to the room and it was up to the student polygraph examiners to decide who committed the crime and who saw him do it — we had to "play dumb" for all questioning. For some reason, one day when I didn't commit the crime, I was in a difficult mood and I set a record on the polygraph machine (complete lying). I'm sure they suspected me of something! (For that reason, I will never take a polygraph exam!) Two months later, I graduated and got orders for Vietnamese Language School at Ft. Bliss, El Paso, TX. As you may surmise, very few folks in Germany know the Vietnamese language!

I spent three months at Ft. Bliss learning Vietnamese (somewhat) in an emersion program taught by a Vietnamese instructor. It turned out that they had sent about a dozen MPs to the language school and we all wondered what they had in mind for us. I opined that, whatever it was, we were screwed. The Vietnamese in the larger cities all knew some English, so they would be sending us out in the boonies to keep 101st Airborne troops away from the local girls. Although that's not necessarily bad duty, I saw major problems in our future in Southeast Asia. Nonetheless, whoever decided to send us to Vietnamese Language School didn't follow through, so when we reached Vietnam, we were assigned as regular MPs. No guarding the girls.

After I arrived at my MP 93rd Battalion headquarters in Qui Nhon, a fellow whom I knew from my first time in MP School ran onto our bus. He hastily asked if I knew how to type. I responded that I could "hunt and peck," and he said that was fine. It turned out that the battalion adjutant's secretary had returned to the states and they needed someone to fill that position. I eagerly grabbed that job! Most of the MPs who arrived with me ended up escorting convoys through the contested Central Highlands of the country, so I considered myself lucky to land the clerk-typist position.

It is worthwhile noting that the only substantive time while I was in-country that I used my Vietnamese was one evening while pulling guard duty by a road next to our compound. Two guys came up to me, said they heard I knew some Vietnamese and asked me to do them a favor. They said that each time they ordered a woman she was always "ugly as hell," and asked me to order them two good-looking women. I said I would do it and yelled to a guy passing by the guard tower on a motor scooter with no woman on the back. The same type scooter is in the VNE Quonset Hut for anyone to see. I asked him to bring two good-looking women to the front gate of the compound in fifteen minutes, but I placed my order in Vietnamese. Considering the language I used, he was shocked! He nodded his head and then drove off to accomplish his mission. I saw the two guys the next morning at chow and asked how it had gone. They each gave me the hand sign for "great!" So, I always say that I pimped for the Army while I was in Vietnam — and yet, didn't get any money for it!

After finishing the Army in 1971 as an E-4, I returned to UConn and completed my PhD in 1974. I taught for 31 years in the biology department at the College of Charleston until 2005. Among the many courses I taught, I focused primarily on teaching about invertebrates on both the undergrad and graduate levels. In addition to doing research along the Carolina coast, I also did studies between Atlanta and Gettysburg, PA, in the Blue Ridge Mountains and at Ascension Island, a small, volcanic island on the equator about midway between Brazil and western Africa. (As a British colony, the island served as the step-off point for British forces during the Falklands War.)

My first stint as a volunteer was as an orderly in the emergency room (ER) at Roper Hospital for four years back in the 1980s. (I pulled a 3-11 shift each Sunday.) One of the most stressful times was immediately after Hurricane Hugo, when guys would use electric chain-saws for the first time — lots of guys were seriously injured and had to come to the ER with some pretty bad injuries. I became a volunteer for Patriots Point in March 2007, wrote the narratives given to our new volunteers for the major things to see on our most popular tours (the hanger deck and tours 1 and 3), did the same for the accompanying "butt cards," oriented new volunteers for a few years, and I've been editor of the volunteer newsletter *Scuttlebutt* since about 2009. Because I had been editing term papers, theses and professional manuscripts for over thirty years and thoroughly enjoy writing, I thought working on *Scuttlebutt* would be something great. Two of my favorite articles have been the Brown-Water Navy and Blimps. With respect to my interaction with visitors, two things have stuck with me. One is how thankful they are for those of us who served in Vietnam. Second is their naïveté about all things military. It is sometimes surprising hoc little information folks know about our armed forces.

My wife, Marty, and I live on James Island. My first wife and I had a small wedding at an Army chapel at Ft. Gordon in 1969 and then got a divorce in the late 1980s. I was then single for many years. Marty and I married in 2005 and have lived in my home since then. Marty is a professional potter, sculptor and painter.

That's about it for me. I'm an Army veteran, a Vietnam War veteran, have a Ph.D. in biology, and I'm a volunteer at the Naval and Maritime Museum at Patriots Point. I enjoy meeting visitors, and enjoy producing *Scuttlebutt.*

Note: I admire Chip's production and distribution of Scuttlebutt, and like most all volunteers, look forward to each issue. Equally enjoyable is his rendition of his experiences in

MP School and as a military policeman in Vietnam. Having taught at the US Army Military Police School at Ft Gordon as a Marine Corps captain, we have a bond. However, as Chip explains his research duties in the Weddell Sea of: . . . *masses of sponge spicules (undecomposable silicon dioxide needles embedded in sponge tissue as an anti-predatory mechanism) and foraminiferans (small, calcareous, unicellular organisms. . .* I must admit I do not fully grasp those maritime duties, other than, he was somewhere south of where we are now, and doing something a little different than what we do here. But, Chip knows what he was doing and that is what is important.

Stoney

CHAPTER 17

VOLUNTEER ANDREW BARRETT

★★★

First of all, what brought me to Patriots Point? Well, I have been visiting here since I was a small boy, and have always had a love and fascination for the ships at Patriots Point. I had numerous relatives that served in WW II. My Great Uncle Cecil was a Marine corporal in an infantry unit, and saw a lot of action in the Pacific. When the HBO mini-series "The Pacific" came out he was in most of that action, and he was around when I was growing up, so, I heard many stories about it from him.

My other Great Uncle Ben (My Grandmother's baby brother) was in Pre-Law at the University of North Carolina, at Chapel Hill, and volunteered, after the bombing of Pearl Harbor took place. He joined the Army Air Corps and was assigned to a B-26 Marauder. He was shot down and killed-in-action during the Battle of Midway.

I started doing WW II reenacting about fifteen years ago, and I am also part of the ***USS North Carolina Living History Crew*** that would come down to Patriots Point and assist in the events for the ***USS Laffey Living History Crew***. I am the new executive officer (XO) of that organization and am trying to beef it back up and, so-far, we are looking good headed in that direction.

I want to do something special next year for the 75th anniversary of D-Day since *Laffey* was there.

I started volunteering at Patriots Point (PP) a few months ago, and once-in-a-while, I will have my reproduction khakis on while setting up in the Wardroom aboard *Yorktown*. And, when the visitors come in, I talk a little about how officers ate, versus how enlisted ate, down below. It is always well received and I believe the public really enjoys the "hands on" experience so they can see items from that time period, and visualize how the wardroom would have looked in 1945.

As far as personal experience, I really enjoy when folks talk about their grandfathers, uncles, brothers, and even their fathers, who served in any capacity during that war. Of course, I also have ladies sometimes talk about their female relatives who served or supported the war efforts. It serves to create a real bond and people are really excited to talk about their ancestors and relatives.

I have all but given up doing Civil War and Revolutionary War reenactments, in order to focus on acting as the XO (executive officer) of the *USS Yorktown / USS Laffey Living History Crew*, as an actor, with others, as well as a volunteer at PP. I am keeping my fingers crossed to be in the proposed Mel Gibson movie about the *Laffey*. I was in one of his other movies (both my wife and myself), and we'll see what happens.

Andrew: Please add more detail about the reenactments, the performances, the actors, etc.

I will be on board *Laffey* on Wednesday's doing living history and talking to the public. How cool would it be to have a volunteer dressed in period garb talking to the public about *Laffey* ?? Cool!

Regards,

Andrew Barrett

CHAPTER 18

VOLUNTEER BILL MILCAREK

★★★

Bill Milcarek: Photo property of author

The mighty B-52 bomber is one of the most deadly weapons in the arsenal of the United States military. For almost sixty years, it has proven itself over and over again by accomplishing and completing a variety of missions through those years.

The "BUFF," an acronym for Big Ugly Fat F***** (some say the last word as Fellow, while others use another word beginning with the letter F) is in the Air Force Operations Plan until 2050. Over its long life, nothing could compare to a series of missions over North Vietnam in December 1972, through early January 1973. For the United States, those missions ended the war in Vietnam.

Briefly, North Vietnam had balked during peace talks in Paris. President Richard Nixon wanted to convince them to return to the table. The B-52 would be the means to that end. In all, a total of 741 B-52 sorties were flown during Operation Linebacker II, between 18 and 29 December 1972 (actually, a little longer than that official end date). Fifteen B-52s were shot down during Line Backer II. During those missions, the B-52s shot down two MIG-21s. Thirty-four B-52 Crewmen were killed in action and thirty-two were taken prisoner by the North Vietnamese Army. Twenty-five BUFF crew members were recovered.

Bill's crew had flown two linebacker missions unscathed but was aboard the last B-52 to be shot down by a SAM (Surface-to-Air Missile) over Vinh, North Vietnam, on 4 Jan 1973. By March 1973, the last American ground combat forces had been withdrawn from South Vietnam. For the United States, the war was over and we had accomplished our mission. The Republic of South Vietnam still stood against onslaughts from the Viet Cong and from North Vietnam. And, President Richard Nixon assured the President of the Republic of South Vietnam that, if the North violated the settlement reached in Paris, the United States "will respond with full force." So, South Vietnam took over the reins in defending themselves.

Linebacker II was designed to achieve a political end. Flying as the copilot of one of the B-52s participating in Operation Linebacker II was one of the youngest pilots in the Air Force, at that time, flying that mighty aircraft with the call-sign *Ruby II.* It was a Model D, B-52 which had a payload of 108 five hundred-pound bombs. He is also a volunteer at the Naval and Maritime Museum at Patriots Point. His name is William Milcarek. Better known by the name of Bill. He was born in Sterling, Illinois, graduated Newman high school in 1965 and Tulane University in 1969. He is not married and has four children; his son is living with his family on Isle of Palms.

I first met Bill at the VFW Post on Isle of Palms, where we briefly talked of his experiences in life, especially during his time co-piloting a B-52 during Operation Linebacker II. Bill was a USAF pilot for ten years flying the B-52D and the C-5A. He currently resides in Mt Pleasant, South Carolina.

After college, Bill received the “Greeting” notice from Uncle Sam to be drafted into the military. Instead, he chose joining the US Air Force to fly jets and was assigned to Undergraduate Flight Training at Webb AFB in Big Springs, Texas. His PCS assignment was in B-52s at Dyess, AFB in Abilene, Texas. Later Bill flew C-5As in the Air Force Reserves out of Dover, Delaware for four years. He was assigned “Temporary Duty” to Guam and Thailand for 470 days. His sorties to North Vietnam were flown out of both Guam and Thailand. From Utapao, Thailand the missions to Vietnam were approximately three-hours flying time; whereas missions from Guam were about twelve-hours flying time.

For the first time in the war, swarms of B-52s dropped thousands of tons of bombs on concentrated military and industrial targets in North Vietnam. Unfortunately, political rather than tactical planners sent in wave after wave of bombers at the same altitude, in the same direction, again and again. Flying straight and level until bombs were released, then making the same directional turn resulting in loss of ECM (Electronic Counter Measures) exposing planes and crews to the deadly Soviet surface-to-air missiles.

Bill’s aircraft was hit by a surface-to-air missile and his aircraft was badly damaged. All flight and engine instruments were made unusable, except the still working altimeter, due to the direct hit by the SAM in the lower left nose of the BUFF. Also, a broken refueling manifold dumped gallons of fuel over the two crew members down below. Ultimately, the crew ejected or bailed-out, landing in the South China Sea off the coast of DaNang, Vietnam, with all crewmen except the navigator managing to eject from the burning, crippled aircraft. Ejecting or bailing out of a fast moving aircraft is a risky maneuver, especially when only a few of the eight engines remained controllable and most of the instruments unworkable from damage by the explosion. Unable to judge forward speed before exiting a falling, fast moving aircraft is a non-habit-forming practice. By skill and luck, they made it to a designated bail-out area about twenty miles off shore, and with extreme difficulty managed to exit the aircraft.

Bill tells the story: *Our mission on 4 Jan 1973 was the target of Vinh just below the 19th parallel in North Vietnam. We flew at 35,000 feet at night. I watched their SAM from launch until it disappeared under the nose of our aircraft. It did not move in the aircraft window which meant it was tracking towards its target—us! The navigator failed to eject in his seat from the aircraft since the SAM warped his hatch. When he activated the ejection system, he only went down about four inches The navigator's ejection system was designed to be ejected downward, out the bottom of the aircraft. Since he had to make a manual bail-out, it caused him serious injury leaving the aircraft flying in excess of an estimated speed of 400 knots.*

We did not have inter-phone communication with the gunner. We would have landed the aircraft if he did not bail out. I learned much later, actually during a lunch at the VFW on Isle of Palms with the actual gunner of that aircraft, that the aircraft was on fire after we were hit. Those of us up-front didn't know that. Actually, as terrifying as it was, it would have made it much more terrifying!

From Nampows.org/B-52.html Website:

Aircraft Ruby 2, B52D, 1-4-73, Anderson AFB, No. 55-0056. SA2 hit over Vinh. Went feet wet, crew bailed out in South China Sea, all rescued by helos from USS Saratoga. P-LtCol Gerald Wickline; Co-P Capt Bill Milcarek; Tail gunner T/Sgt Carlos S. Killgore; NAV Capt Myles McTernan; R/Nav Maj. Robt. A. Klingheil; EWO Capt. Wm. E. Ferg. (Combat loss, 7).

Bill tried getting an airline pilot position, but when he got out of the Air Force there was a glut of pilots looking for a job. Some had been furloughed from their Airline job for ten or more years. Bill had a family to support so he found a job as an Aviation Underwriter in New York City where his wife already had a job as a fashion model.

After a few years in the New York Market, I was offered an international Reinsurance Underwriting position, which included involvement in Aviation and Space portfolios. Actually, to this day I continue as an Advisory Board Member for Aviation and Space for a semiconductor disruptive technology start-up company.

After about a year in New York, one of my B-52 pilot buddies called me up from Dover, Delaware and said the C-5 unit there was looking for pilots with B-52 experience because they know how to air-refuel. My civilian boss thought it would be a good idea and gave me three months leave of absence to learn to fly C-5s in Altus, Oklahoma.

Bill vividly remembers the first time he released the brakes on a C-5 for take-off. He never thought he would be flying huge aircraft again once he got out of the Air Force.

Bill had ten years Air Force duty. Just over Five years active, and just short of five years reserve time. He began his volunteer work at Patriots Point in March of 2018. Bill relates: *I enjoy being a volunteer and have had some interesting experiences with visitors to the Naval and Maritime Museum. One in particular was hearing from an F-15 engineer who was visiting the museum, about an aircraft part being "borrowed" from the front landing gear of our F-15 on the deck of the Yorktown to replace a faulty part on an active F-15. Talk about an acute shortage of parts in the active forces. That's one for the books.*

CHAPTER 19

ABOUT VOLUNTEER BILL WATKINSON, JR.

★★★

The following narratives are the thoughts, words, and experiences of one of the many volunteers at the Naval and Maritime Museum at Patriots Point, South Carolina where, among other duties, he drives the shuttle, often on Saturday. In that capacity as a shuttle driver, he gets to meet many interesting people as he drives them down that long causeway from the museum entrance to the "Fighting Lady," USS *Yorktown*. Well! Let's let him tell the story:

"Most of the visitors riding on my cart, I get to see and hear their comments only one time, one ride down to the carrier; however, a few of those, very few, I catch on a return trip from the carrier back to the entrance of the museum. All are different. Most are interesting comingled with some who are perhaps mundane. For the most part they are simply every-day, ordinary people paying a visit to the naval museum at Patriots Point; however, some are very interesting to briefly chat with. Then, there are the smaller few of these visitors, and most of those volunteers, riding my cart are, in a word, extraordinary. Just listening and talking with them exposes backgrounds, exploits, and experiences landing in the historically significant category. I get to meet and greet, chat with, joke with, and interact with some of these extraordinary people. It makes my duties interesting, and sometimes challenging in my volunteer positions. I'd like to relate the story of just one person in particular who rides my shuttle.

"Early-on, I met and transported an awe-inspiring individual, a fellow Volunteer. He enters my shuttle cart along with a constant care-giving companion almost every Saturday, six or seven months a year for a ride to *Yorktown*. Another Volunteer meets them at the gangway to escort them to the hanger deck. There, he sits near the World War-II, F-6-F Hellcat Navy fighter aircraft and meets with, and talks with any visitor interested in his story, and his stories are captivating. He especially loves to talk with the youngsters, those young Americans who will someday perhaps take his place in the annals of naval aviation. He remains at that place, in that position for a couple of hours or more, and then, almost reluctantly, he reverses his path aboard and returns to my shuttle whereupon I deliver him and his companion back to their car in the parking lot. This ninety-six-year-old Navy veteran of World War II, a volunteer at this museum, who loves flying and talking about flying, is one of just a few of these vanishing icons in our group of volunteers at this naval museum.

"Now, let me tell you what I have learned about this World War II Navy fighter pilot, from conversations with his fellow volunteers, from previous writings of and about him, and from brief conversations with him through the years as we travelled back and forth on that causeway. He was born in Blawknox, Pennsylvania and graduated from high school in that fateful year of 1941. Then, he entered Bucknell University in the fall of that year. On the day before the "Day of Infamy," On 6 December he and his future bride, Gladys Benfield, went on their first date, a college dance, not knowing that on the next day, fate would intervene delaying their romance and their marriage until 23 November 1946. Like thousands of other young men, he joined the United States Navy immediately after the United States declared war on Japan.

"The Navy had plans for him, but, they wanted him to finish one more year of college and then to attend boot camp and enter the Navy's flying program. For him, that flying program began in November 1942, almost a year after he enlisted. It didn't take them long to realize he was a good pilot, perhaps even an extraordinary pilot. As a result, he was eventually chosen as a test-pilot, test-flying new aircraft right out of the factory, and also became a much needed ferry pilot getting Navy aircraft from the factory to where they were desperately needed. Also, he ferried damaged aircraft sent from the Pacific to the US west coast and would ferry them back to the east coast for necessary repairs. The ferrying of aircraft was critical to the war effort. All-the-while, he continued to go through various training modules and routine transfers to various duty stations growing his skills. He excelled in gaining flying experience by flying numerous types of Navy aircraft, honing skills that would eventually be transferrable to new pilots entering the naval air arm. He was becoming one hell of an outstanding aviator. Today, he can boast that he had flown every model of propeller aircraft currently on the hanger deck of *Yorktown* except the AD Skyraider and B-25 Mitchell.

"Once, he actually met and had a long conversation with the famous aviator Charles Lindbergh as both of them were ferrying aircraft for the Navy. Because of his vast experience and his remarkable eyesight, he eventually ended up flying night-fighters. You had to be a top-notch pilot for that assignment. His first carrier-flying occurred in October 1944 aboard USS *Sable*, a converted side-wheel steamer on Lake Michigan. From February through April 1945, he had advanced night-fighter and carrier training in the F-6-F and F-6-F-N (night) Hellcat fighters and, in April joined Combat Air Pool Squadron VF-99 flying escort for bombers and bombing Japanese defensive positions, mostly at night. Finally, in May 1945, he was transferred to Air Group-9 aboard *Yorktown*, the same ship currently docked at Patriots Point. The same ship he boards most every Saturday to sit and talk of flying in war and peace.

"From *Yorktown*, he flew F-6-F-N fighters conducting combat air patrols at night. He can vividly describe nighttime carrier landings and take-offs saying that he actually preferred the nighttime operations to daytime flying. On one mission during the battle for Okinawa, his aircraft was hit damaging a wing and his landing gear. Unable to retract his dropped landing gear, and with one wing shot to pieces, he made a dangerous, but successful landing aboard *Yorktown's* crowded deck. With a replacement landing gear, and a new wing installed, the aircraft was ready to fly the next day.

He was flying combat air patrol along the coast of Japan when the surrender documents were signed aboard the Battleship USS *Missouri* in Tokyo Bay.

"In June 1947, he returned to Bucknell to complete those studies interrupted by the war. Bucknell offered a flying course, and he took it. It didn't take his flying instructor long to find out that his student was, by far, the better pilot. During his time at Bucknell, he also ferried supplies to a hunting camp, and after graduating, he joined the Navy Reserve Combat Squadron VF-96A at Floyd Bennett Field, which was part of the Naval Air Station, New York from the beginning of World War II through the 1960s. He was activated to active duty for the Korean War, serving in stateside duties involving flying. Then, he joined Eastern Airlines. He retired from Eastern Airlines in 1982, when he reached the mandatory retirement age for commercial pilots; however, he continued to fly and kept flying aircraft of all types until his late 80s. He has, for over 60 years, been an active flying pilot.

"Briefly, this has been the life of this man, this Patriots Point Volunteer, Bill Watkinson, Jr. a retired from flying, lifetime pilot. Bill now lives in Flemington, NJ, and Charleston, SC, on a 50/50 basis. He became a Patriots Point Volunteer in February 2014 at ninety-one years of age. He is one of our senior Volunteers. His stated goal is to tell the young people of today about something they don't teach in school today. It's about the youngsters of World War II. Those daring young men in their flying machines, young men who rose to the challenge in time of war to disrupt and defeat rogue nations attempting to enslave the world. He also relates to today's visiting aviation enthusiast, telling them intimate details about the propeller driven aircraft of the days of yore, and the daring young men who flew them. Yes, men of that generation still have a story to tell and he intends to tell it—as long as he possibly can.

"Bill Watkinson is a Patriots Point Volunteer. As I was thinking of how to more adequately describe Bill to the reader of this anthology, for some unexplained reason the lines of the poem *High Flight* by John Gillespie Magee, Jr., kept whispering to me, again and again. Interestingly, this poem, written with some of these words, is the way I would describe Bill:

"Oh! I have slipped the surly bonds of earth,

And danced the skies on laughter-silvered wings;

Sunward I've climbed, and joined the tumbling mirth

Of sun-split clouds, --and done a hundred things . . .

(The lines of the poem continue; however, for brevity, I have omitted them)

And, while with silent lifting mind I've trod

The high un-trespassed sanctity of space,

Put out my hand, and touched the face of God."

Thanks to John Gillespie Magee, Jr., for penning such an amazing poem that beautifully describes Bill. Thanks to Connie Reynolds & to Bill Watkinson, Jr., for the many brief conversations and thanks to Chip Biernbaum for providing background information from archived *Scuttlebutt* publications and finally, to Dick West for reading and correcting some of my earlier writings of Bill. Semper Fi all!

Stoney

ACKNOWLEDGEMENTS

This book could not have been completed without the assistance of my wife, Lyn. She has assisted me in my previous book publications and my various magazine articles for *Marine Corps Gazette, Leatherneck,* and *Police Chief.* In addition, she always scans and edits all my writings for various Opinion Page newspaper articles through the years. Needless to admit, she is really the beacon I followed through the writing night.

I am grateful to Jim Vickers for assisting me with photographs, and to Chip Biernbaum for providing "Scuttlebutt" information from his archives. Certainly thanks to our CEO Mac, for the Foreword and his support in many areas.

However, for this specific publication, I also had the day-to-day assistance of our Volunteer Coordinator at the Naval and Maritime Museum, Dick West. Dick guided me to our CEO and set up my appointment for gaining the approval of Mac Burdette. Important though that was, it was his encouragement of the many volunteers to make contact with me and provide their stories for publishing. Without Dick, it would have been next to impossible. Lounge room sea stories, ad lib war tales, and humorous military antidotes are one thing, but when it's revealed that you are going to publish these events as true renderings of people's lives, it does give pause to many.

I found out, as time went by that Dick too had a story or two. Day-by-day, in sometimes cryptic fashion, he related these snippets of his life to me.

Dick West: Photo property of author

★★★

Dick died in December 2018. These conversations with me are related in his honor. R.I.P.

★★★

Dick West was a volunteer, and is now our volunteer coordinator. After encouraging him to provide me with some information that we could place in the book *Short Rations From Patriots Point Volunteers*, the following was gleaned from numerous brief conversations:

Dick was born on June 13, 1945, in Tampa, Florida. He and his Mother were staying with her parents while his Dad was flying the "hump" from Burma to China as a flight engineer in C-46 cargo planes. Dick's Dad ended up participating in three wars, WWII, Korea and Vietnam. With a Dad in the service, the family lived in many places but mainly in Florida and southern Georgia.

Dick had a unique experience in 1951 and 1952. His Dad was in Japan working on B-29s, flying bombing missions over Korea during the Korean War. At one point, the Air Force allowed families to join the servicemen in Japan. Dick and his mother traveled across country via train from Tampa to Seattle, Washington. From there they boarded a US Navy transport for the two-week trip across the Pacific. Even at six-years-old, he still remembers how high the waves were and how sea-sick he got. They spent about a year at Yakota Air Force Base before returning to the USA.

Dick spent his high school days in Albany, Georgia, since his Dad was stationed at Turner Air Force Base there. His dad worked on C-130s but the main function of the base was housing a B-52 squadron. The way things were back then, when the B-52s scrambled, you thought it was just an exercise but in the back of your mind you knew we might actually be at war.

Dick wanted to go to Auburn University on a Navy scholarship and study Aerospace Engineering. He then wanted to fly for the Navy. He had to take a difficult test and the Navy was taking the top 250. Dick was # 251 and first alternate. No one dropped out so he went to the University of

Florida and eventually went through advanced Army ROTC. Florida only had Army and Air Force ROTC and the Air Force wanted four years of his life and the Army just two, so the Army sounded good. Dick eventually found that he did not like Aerospace Engineering and transferred to Construction Management. He often wonders how that one wrong answer on that test changed the entire direction of his life—he went to Florida instead of Auburn, went in the Army instead of the Navy and ended up in Construction Management instead of Aerospace Engineering. He also met his future wife of fifty-one years at Florida and, of course, would not have met her at Auburn. If he had become a Navy pilot, he would have been flying over Vietnam in the 1968 to 1970 time-frame, when we were losing a bunch of Navy pilots. That one wrong answer might have also saved his life.

He met his future wife, Pamela Edds (Pam preceded Dick in death only scant months earlier), at the University of Florida in another odd "chance." He and his fraternity brothers had just finished painting a fixing-up fraternity house (Pi Kappa Alfa). Dick and his roommate had showered and set up the TV. They flipped a coin to see which one would go downstairs to the car and get the TV programs out of the car. Dick lost. As he was walking across the lawn with nothing but Bermuda shorts on, another fraternity brother called Dick over to meet four girls in a car who were "cruising fraternity row." He met Pam and you could say it was love at first sight. He went to change clothes, and then they went out for a coke. They started dating, and in June of 1966 they were married. Much like the one bad answer on the Navy exam changing the direction of his life, if he had not lost the flip of the coin that night, he never would have met his future wife, Pam.

Those of us old enough remember what it was like to be a male back then in the early and mid-1960s, chances are, you were going in the military, or college, or to a paying job; however, soon the Vietnam War started up. That threw a different wrinkle into a young man's life. With his Dad being career Air force, there never was any thought of trying to stay out of the military. He wisely thought it better to go to war as an officer than a private, so he went through Advance Army ROTC. He was commissioned a 2nd Lieutenant in the Army Corps of Engineers the day he graduated in March 1968. He went to Engineer Officer training at Ft. Belvoir, Virginia, and then his first assignment as a Construction Engineer in the headquarters of a Construction Battalion at FT. Stewart, Georgia (Camp Swampy) near Savannah. He was not there very long (about seven months) but, while there, he was involved with the reconstruction of the tank and helicopter gunnery ranges at FT. Stewart. These were ranges where tankers and chopper pilots trained before heading for Vietnam. He received orders for Vietnam in November 1968. The battalion commander, a full colonel, contacted Army Headquarters and told them that Lieutenant West was too important in his job with the Construction Battalion to go to Vietnam. He was, after all, building gunnery ranges to train pilots and tankers who were going to Vietnam. Army Headquarters promptly told the battalion commander to "mind his own business." In short, Dick was off to Vietnam on 9 February 1969. Those of us who went to Vietnam always remember the day you got there because it made all the senses come alive, and you started thinking about the day you would come home.

I vividly recall his conversation about Vietnam, for obvious reasons. We are Vietnam Veterans. He said to me, "Like most of us who went to Vietnam without a specific assignment, went to the Replacement Center at Bien Hua Air Base. I was told I could be there as much as a week before someone figured out what to do with me. I put my bags down on the bunk, and immediately a private appeared asking if I was Lieutenant West. He said, 'Come with me, Sir.' He drove me to Engineer Headquarters at Long Binh where I met with a full colonel. He told me they had been waiting two months for me to get there. It is typical of the Army to leave a guy wondering what in the world his assignment will be in a war zone when they have known for two months. I was assigned as a Construction Officer in USAECAV, the acronym for the US Army Engineer Construction Agency Vietnam, which was based at Army Headquarters at Long Binh. This agency authorized and monitored major construction on major bases being built by the civilian contractors. Though based at Long Binh, I had to travel to the different bases for our projects to observe progress and 'trouble-shoot.' We did this traveling by being flown in a twin engine Beach Craft the Army had purchased and designated a C-21. I was in this job for my entire year in Vietnam, which was unusual. Usually, they rotated you to a different job after six months.

As we met often, Dick would verbally relate snippets of his life before Patriots Point: "I learned something in my work there that I used throughout my Construction Management career. We had a project at Cam Ran Bay that had been stalled for a year because of disagreements between the parties involved. It was so bad no one was even talking to the other. I was sent to Cam Ran Bay to straighten things out. I called a meeting with all of the parties involved in a large conference room. We had about twenty people there. I told them we were going around the room and everyone would have a chance to discuss the problem and how to solve it. I wanted no interruptions because everyone would have an equal chance to talk. We did just that and each person in turn talked. Before we got half way around the room, I heard people start to saying things like 'I did not know he felt like that, I could work with that,' and 'I think that would work,' and 'I have no problem with that,' Soon the people were talking among themselves, working out the year-long problems. That meeting solved the issues and got the project going again. I was viewed as a hero and I did nothing more than get people to talk. They solved the problem themselves once they agreed to sit around a table, face to face, and discuss it. I learned so much from that experience. All of my career, when faced with some insurmountable problem, I would call everyone in from where they were to the same city and have them face each other and discuss the problem. Often I told the people to cancel their return plane tickets and get a hotel room because we are not leaving this city until the problem is resolved. Fortunately, I could do this because I was the boss. When told they could not go home that day, it usually took only a few hours to resolve the problem. That one thing I learned as a lieutenant in the Army, proved useful my whole career.

"My only close call in this war zone was the first month I was there when Tet 1969 rolled around. It was not as serious as Tet 1968; but our base was attacked by ground forces and rockets about 2:30 in the morning. Two rockets went over my building and blew up in the court yard. One fell short and blew up a bus parked next to my building. That was the night I learned I could run a 100 feet on a rock road in my bare feet and not feel a thing. It is amazing what adrenalin can do.

"One particular incident sticks in my pocket of Vietnam remembrances. Part of my job, while traveling to the different bases was looking for unauthorized construction projects. I made one trip up north, about as far north as you can go and still be in South Vietnam. I was met at the plane by the base engineer. He seemed mad at me so I asked him why he was mad because we had never met. He said it was because we had authorized the construction of an Officer Club. I told him there was no such project, and to show it to me. He did. It was a club that an officer was having built with unauthorized funds, a posh building for himself and his buddies. It had central air conditioning, a cut stone fire place, mahogany bar and flush toilets. The hospital there did not even have flush toilets. I came back to Long Binh and wrote up a report which my colonel signed and passed on. It resulted in a lot of brass going up and investigating. It turned out he was apparently redirecting materials and funding from enlisted men's barracks and mess hall projects. Soon all investigations stopped. I asked my boss why it stopped. We had this guy dead to rights. He told me the [name and identification omitted] was a buddy of our big boss and big boss had ordered all investigations to stop. When my time in Vietnam was up, I was put in for the bronze star for meritorious service. It went all the way to the top and my big boss turned it down. His pay-back to me was in the format of our once a month gathering for all men departing for home. All of the headquarters command met to say good-by to those of us going home. The big boss would talk to each person and tell where they were going. He got to me and loudly proclaimed, 'And here we have Lieutenant West. Lieutenant West is getting out of the Army. You don't like the Army, do you Lieutenant West.' Fortunately I did not say a thing. My immediate boss, with tears in his eyes, later apologized for the Army. I got in trouble for just doing my job. I still have an affinity for my time in the Army. I learned much about construction. I still like the Army. It's assholes I don't like.

"I came home February 9, 1970, and immediately was discharged from the Army. I found a job with a very small construction company in Coral Gables, Florida, and started my career as a Construction Manager there. The career path I followed might seem strange to some. I started with small companies with small projects and then went to medium size companies with medium size projects and so on until I worked for huge international companies and managed huge projects. The first half of my career, I build shopping malls, department stores, office buildings, hotels, and some warehouses. The most fun I had was building the Waverly Hotel in Atlanta. It is a 530 room fourteen-story luxury atrium hotel with 531,000 sq. ft. We built it from start of construction to actually opening the hotel in 15½ months, finishing three months early. The owner made a ton of money opening three months early and then gave my company three more projects as a reward.

"At the start of the last part of my career, I got involved in sports facilities. My staff directed the construction of the Atlanta Braves 15,000 seat Minor League stadium in Richmond, Virginia. We tore down the old stadium and built a new one on the same site in 7½ months, during the winter, between baseball seasons. The local newspaper editor marveled at the speed of construction and stated he could not even get a garage built next to his house in 7½ months let alone a stadium.

"I then went on to work on the Atlanta Committee for the Olympic Games (ACOG), managing the design and construction of several sports venues including the aquatic center and the tennis center among others.

I then went on to direct the construction of the Tennessee Titans, NFL football stadium in Nashville, Tennessee and the Philadelphia Eagles, NFL football stadium in Philadelphia.

"One interesting thing happened at the first football game in the Titans Stadium. It was an exhibition game before the season, but a sold-out one. One thing most stadiums test once construction is completed is the ability of the water system and sewer system being able to handle every toilet being flushed at the same time. Stadiums are unique in this respect. At half time, you can expect every toilet to be flushed at one time. The way you test this is called a 'flush off' where you bring in boy and girls scouts to man every toilet in the stadium and, on signal, flush them the same time. We did this and everything worked. We were therefore, surprised on opening night when there was not enough water pressure to operate the toilets on the upper seating deck. This was serious because I had to send my staff up to tell 22,000 people that their toilets were not working and they could not use them. One of my staff came back and told me never to make him do that again. He said to me, 'Do you know that it is like telling women they cannot use the toilet? They were going to throw me off of the upper deck.' We spent days trying to figure out what was wrong because there was another game the next weekend. First our construction was blamed and then the design was blamed. In the end we found that the problem had been the city water department had not had sufficient pressure in their lines to properly service the upper deck of the stadium. They never admitted this, of course, but nothing was changed on the stadium and they have never had that problem again.

"After the Eagles Stadium project, my company, Turner Construction Company, coerced me into working overseas. I worked a month in Jeddah Saudi Arabia and could not stand it, so I opted for another assignment. I thought I would be there for a while so I looked for housing. In Saudi everyone lived in compounds. The Americans had a compound, the English had a compound, etc. I went to the American Compound which had a very nice apartment the company would rent for me. The compound had a ten-foot high concrete wall around it and barbed wire on the top. At the entrance gate there sat a manned Saudi tank. I thought if they had to have a tank at the entrance, things must be serious here.

"I then went to Dubai which is a much more civilized place. You can drink there! I was to manage two construction management teams working for Nahkeel a government owned development-company. Our first task was to "save" a $250 million shopping-mall project. The first construction manager had fallen way behind schedule and was fired. We had to finish the project on schedule. To do so meant we had to put in place an average of $20 million in construction per month for ten months. In this country, that is unheard of for a project that size, mainly because they cannot find enough people. In Dubai there is a huge amount of workers imported from China, Bangladesh, the Philippines, etc. At one time, we had as many as 4,000 workers on this project. In comparison, the most workers I ever had a NFL stadium project was about 1,500 workers. We did complete the project on time. The second team was tasked with building 2,500 luxury condominium units in thirteen buildings on the trunk of 'Palm Island.' This is the Island they created to look like a palm tree by dredging sand from under the water and creating the Island. We never could figure out the true cost of the project, but it was well over a billion dollars. Dubai was amazing for any construction guy. It looked like a forest of tower cranes. When I was there, they estimated that 20 percent of all tower cranes in the world were in Dubai. The only down side to Dubai was the heat. In July and August it typically was as high as 127 degrees. Four of us actually played nine holes of golf when it was 127 degrees. On the third hole we thought we had made a huge mistake but we did finish. By the way, there was also humidity because Dubai is on the coast.

"I got tired of being so far away from home, so I took a job with Destination Development Company, as subsidiary of Lowe Enterprises that owns Wild Dunes Resort on the Isle of Palms, South Carolina. My wife and I moved from Atlanta to Mount Pleasant in the summer of 2005. My first assignment was to manage the design and construction of a new conference center and the Villages, a condominium complex. My overall job as a Vice President was to oversee all of their development on the east coast since they are based in LA. The only other project they were developing on the east coast, at the time, was a condominium complex at the Stowe, Vermont Ski Resort so I got to fly up there a lot. Unfortunately in 2008, the recession came along and Lowe laid-off their entire development and construction team, since no one was buying condominiums any longer.

"While unsuccessfully looking for a job, I decide I needed to do something so I started to volunteer at Patriots Point. I soon did find a job working for the Seminole Hard Rock Hotel and Casino operation in Florida. I was to manage the design and construction of a $900 million addition to their Tampa Hotel and Casino. After five months of that, the bank withdrew their financing due to the economy, so I was again out of a job. I came back to volunteering. Though I did have some close calls on interesting jobs, including a new Australian Football and Soccer stadium in Perth, Australia, nothing came through.

"After volunteering for six years, I was hired as a part-time docent. The next year, Mac Burdette decided the volunteer program needed a full-time coordinator and increased funding, so he hired me to run the program and I have enjoyed every minute of it. As a volunteer or docent, I did not know a lot of the volunteers. Once I took over the program, I had to know all of the volunteers. I then realized that we have a very unique and special group of people volunteering at Patriots Point. It has been a rewarding experience for me being involved with such a fine group of people."

★★★

So, as you see, Dick has a very interesting background. I am eternally grateful for his personal assistance in this publication, and cherish his stories told to me. Dick told me that he has never seen such a magnificent group of people as are the Volunteers of Patriots Point. "They are unique," he says, "military, civilian, men, and women. They are amazing." Since I am one of them, I will totally agree with Dick.

Ralph Stoney Bates

> ** As this book was in the long publishing process, Dick West passed away from an illness in late December 2018. He will be missed. "Rest in peace, soldier brave. God is nigh." **

Dick West Memorial

ABOUT THE EXECUTIVE EDITOR/CONTRIBUTING AUTHOR OF THIS ANTHOLOGY:

I am Ralph Stoney Bates, Sr., retired from the United States Marine Corps in 1981, and also retired from the Broward County (FL) Sheriff's Office, in 1997. After retiring from the United States Marine Corps and later from the position of deputy sheriff in Florida, I entered into the fascinating world of writing. Proudly, I am the author of three books, *Short Rations For Marines,* an anthology of true stories of Marines and/or Fleet Marine Force sailors, or their immediate family, *A Marine Called Gabe*: the life and times of John Archer Lejeune, the thirteenth Commandant of the Marine Corps, and *An American Shame: the Abandonment of an Entire American Population,* about the Chamorros of Guam and their defiance of the Japanese occupiers during World War II.

Also, I am an assisting-author of *Back Step,* a military-si-fi—historical fiction whose author died before he could finish his manuscript. He had written the manuscript, over time, in the 1980s. His step-daughter commissioned me and my wife to finish and rework the aged and yellowed papers. When it was finished by my wife, Lyn, and me, his step-daughter published that book. All these books are sold through Amazon.com. In addition I am the author of several articles for the *Marine Corps Gazette* and *Leatherneck* magazines, and an article in the *Police Chief* magazine, plus numerous opinion editorials (OpEd's) with several newspapers spanning more than 30 years. These opinion editorials are usually around Veterans Day and/or Memorial Day.

By volunteering at Patriots Point, it serves many reasons and many goals. Chief among them is my desire to devote my time in the service of others. Patriots Point Naval and Maritime Museum offers that reachable goal. The opportunity to meet visitors from all States and Territories, and from all over the world, and to tell them the story of America through the eyes of those who have devoted their blood, sweat, and tears in the service of their country through military service, or support work in the defense industry, is a noble calling. Although it is not necessary for a volunteer to be a former or current military service person to tell the story of those living and dead members of the armed forces of the United States of whom and for whom this museum exists, it does give them an edge. However, it is only necessary for a volunteer to make an effort, in some way, to tell the stories of our heroes, utilizing as a backdrop, the visible displays this museum offers. My goal is simple. To be a vessel of delivery in conjuring the intangibles of duty, honor, and sacrifice into the tangible men and women who actually walked the steps of heroes aboard and upon these visible artifacts of this museum. To make them live in the memories of our visitors as best I can.

Life is a series of happenings, planned and unplanned, that moves us in this race called human toward a destination with immortality. We leave something of ourselves with every person we encounter and we take something from each person that stays with us forever— good, bad or indifferent. I have been a Marine since the age of seventeen with twenty-six years active duty, and a law enforcement officer (deputy sheriff) for sixteen years, with two Sheriff's Departments. During that time, especially during my Marine Corps active duty, I encountered hundreds, if not thousands, of people involved in events one could describe as an event full of sorrow, excitement, horror, fun, rage, comfort and perhaps a dozen other situational adjectives. Many, if not all, of these events could be described in either a small sentence or paragraph, while others could fill a book, telling the story in flowing details.

This is not new to me. My first publication of a book is *Short Rations For Marines*, an anthology which encompassed two-and-a-half years of collecting, cajoling and encouraging Marines, Fleet Marine Force Sailors and/or those who knew them best, to come forward with a segment of their life and immortalize it in print. It is a collection of true short stories covering the everyday lives of Marines, Fleet Marine Force Sailors and/or their families. It spans several generations and wars. But, it is not full of war stories, nor full of human interest stories. It is a good balance of both.

On page vii, of "Short Rations." titled Acknowledgements, I penned the following passage: ***I wish to acknowledge all the authors who presented their stories to record and also to those who have a story or more to tell but hesitated to have them immortalized in print.*** Over forty contributors' submitted stories, but only thirty-five contributors had agreed to have them included in the book. However, after the book was published, and released, with these thirty-five contributors submitting fifty-two stories printed between the cover, I received a flood of stories arriving too late for inclusion in the anthology *Short Rations For Marines.* Thus, my acknowledgement.

After accepting a position as a volunteer at Patriots Point in July 2017, I have read of, overheard, and been a participant in numerous conversations, with, of, and between volunteers. Sometimes it's just idle conversations, sometimes while discussing specific events, and sometimes it's simply being close enough to overhear stories of events, activities, and individuals. These conversations were often related to their previous profession(s), sometimes from their duties as a volunteer, and sometimes a combination of the two. It didn't take me long to realize what a unique group we have in these volunteers at this museum. As a writer, I reasoned, if those stories were combined into an anthology, it would reflect great credit upon them as individual volunteers, and to the organization for whom they volunteer. This idea has been with me for a lengthy period of time, so I had a conversation with some of the "big folks" in our organization that went something like this:

From my observations and discussions on volunteer trips, dinners, and "on duty" at the Museum, stories float between individuals that are not just interesting, but tell of significant events and of individuals within those events that will be lost in the shadowed recesses of the dust-bin of history, if not told to the public via some medium. It is my desire to offer that medium. The goal of this new endeavor is to highlight the background, dedication, loyalty, and significance of the many volunteers of Patriots Point in similar fashion as my book *Short Rations For Marines* highlighted so many Marines and sailors to the delight of spouses, children, grandchildren, friends, and the reading public. Many of these stories became inspirations for others. I wanted to replicate my first anthology with one from these volunteers. Hopefully, the Naval and Maritime Museum through its Bookstore/Gift-Shop may benefit the Yorktown Foundation via supporting this anthology.

Permission was granted by the CEO, and I proceeded.

★★★

As previously mentioned, during my years as an active duty Marine, I encountered many tragic, humorous, sad, outlandish, and life-changing events that compile a large portion of my life and they still dwell within me even today. One in particular was the death of my cousin, Frank Kitchens. As a Marine Lance Corporal, he was killed in combat in Vietnam. I had the sad duty and enriched honor of escorting his body home to his young bride for burial with honor. I had never met her, but Frank had told me so much about her, I felt I did. It was an experience that, though occurring almost fifty years ago, remains as a sharp sadness, combined with intense pride that will never fade.

From receiving the notification of his death by gunfire while on patrol in Vietnam, throughout the four-day event, and on to returning to my home from the location of his funeral, I will never forget the sad, moving, and yet prideful experience. I wrote a story about that experience in the anthology *Short Rations For Marines.* The title of my story was "Under The Apple Tree."

Like most of our volunteers, I've had a whole lot of diverse experiences as an active duty Marine. Many good ones, some sad ones, a few "pucker factor" ones, and some down-right funny, or odd-ball ones. But, as years go by, I tend to dwell on the more humorous, or odd-ball events over and over again. From that genus most of my memories survive and thrive. I'll relate just one more (can't resist the temptation) of my favorite "lighter" times. It was as a Drill Instructor at Parris Island.

I was a sergeant when I attended Drill Instructors School in 1959. The Marine Corps also introduced the new ranks of Lance Corporal, Master Gunnery Sergeant, and Gunnery Sergeant, moving from seven enlisted pay grades to nine around the same time. Actually, as Marine Corps rank structure changed, and brown (cordovan) shoes, emblems on the shirt collar, and stenciled chevrons on sleeves of utility shirts disappeared, my three-stripe sergeant rank became an "Acting" Sergeant (without crossed rifles). Suddenly, with a stroke of a pen, an E-4 sergeant became equivalent to an E-4 corporal (with crossed rifles). But, in its unquestionable infinite wisdom, the Marine Corps didn't suddenly make all of us sergeants a corporal. Instead, all ranks above corporal E- 3, became "Acting." Corporals, sergeants, staff sergeants, etc., thus, we became "Acting" (that rank).

Anyhow, back to the story. I was a Drill Instructor from 1959 through 1961, with an eight-month hiatus as a military policeman in early 1961. My duties were with K Company of the 2nd Recruit Training Battalion at Parris Island, until assigned to Guard Company of Headquarters Battalion as a military policeman. Then later, recalled to DI duty in late

1961, assigned to I Company, of the same battalion. Sometime in 1960, we were picking-up a new platoon of recruits from Recruit Receiving. Tom (last name omitted) a staff sergeant (acting) was the senior DI, and we were joined by a brand new corporal right out of DI School. Not an acting one, instead, a real one, an E-4 corporal. This corporal must and will remain anonymous until the statute of limitations on stupidity runs its course.

This guy looked like he had jumped off a Marine Corps recruiting poster, all squared away and as eager as kid in an ice cream store with a pocket full of dollars. Making a long story as short as possible, this corporal was an overly eager, over bearing, somewhat unsure of himself, and covering it up with bravado, junior drill instructor, as stated, right out of DI School. He was always volunteering to "take care" of anything needed to be taken care of, always "sucking up" to Tom.

We were still in the "shock and control" stage of training a recruit platoon when we began to notice this particular recruit. Keeping with the identity secrets in this story, let's call him "Dynamite." He was unusual to say the least. He was sharp, motivated, disciplined, and, get this, unafraid. Something that was even more unusual was—we did not and could not intimidate him. The more you pushed him, the more he excelled. Once we had the platoon on toes and elbows, a rather painful position to be in, and, like the locker-box manual of arms—we used it sparingly. It didn't take thirty seconds until every recruit quickly dropped off their elbows reclining their entire body to the deck, except Dynamite. He was still on his toes and elbows with no other part of his body touching the deck. I had just stepped over him about to yell out for all these prone recruits to get to the position of attention when, at the same time, I turned and yelled at Dynamite, still on toes and elbows, "Are you hurting, maggot!"

Not quivering a bit, he responded, "Sir, no Sir!"

"Do you feel pain, maggot?"

Gritting his teeth, he again responded, "Sir, no Sir." As I turned my back to him I could hear, "Pain is good, Sir," he added, in a hushed whisper. Faint, but I heard it. I walked away from him suppressing a smile only to hear an unusual loud groan behind me. I turned to see Corporal Poster Marine standing upright on this recruits back. Dynamite was now quivering but still on toes and elbows.

I had to act to stop this abuse without giving away DI secrets, and diminishing the corporal in presence of recruits. "Corporal, (name) get me the index file from the DI House," I stated matter-of-factly. He hesitated, still standing on this recruits back. "Now!" I said, looking directly into his eyes. I jerked my head toward the DI House. He stepped off the recruit and walked toward the DI House which was a room off the passageway outside the squadbay. It's where the DI's worked from, and slept in when on duty throughout the night. Calling all the recruits to the position of attention, I followed. Once inside the DI House and out of view of the squadbay full of our recruits, I pointed my finger an inch from his face and loudly exclaimed.

"Don't do that to recruits. You know better. You'll get all of us in trouble."

As time went by, there were other small things, and a couple of rule violation things that he did which irritated me through the next few days. Unquestionably, he had targeted Dynamite for special attention harassment.

The straw broke the camel's back one dark morning when I had the platoon at breakfast. As usual, Dynamite was the first to finish the meal and fell into formation outside reading his red *Guidebook For Marines,* when I look out the window and see this "Poster Marine" corporal walk up and slap the guidebook out of Dynamite's hands. Dynamite went immediately to the position of attention. Our stalwart corporal then begins to scream into his face and punch him in the chest with his finger. Poster boy was yelling that he was going to fit Dynamite with a "blue suit." At Parris Island, at that time, everyone knew what that meant. I walked out to the almost reformed platoon formation and told the corporal to go in and have his meal while I took the platoon back to the barracks.

The senior and I had a long conversation about this corporal with a vast difference of opinion. Tom thought the corporal was "trying too hard," but would turn out okay, "Just needs close supervision for a while," he surmised. I thought otherwise. Tom also thought that Dynamite was a psychologically imbalanced recruit. I also thought otherwise on that subject. But, since Tom was senior, his view prevailed.

Dynamite took all the abuse the corporal threw at him. Sometimes Tom would step in to correct the corporal, and I was often stepping in to the point that Tom actually told me once to "lay off." the corporal.

Marine Corps recruit training is tough. Some recruits never make it into the first training cycle for several reasons, often included as one of the reasons is the authority of the Psychiatric Observation Unit (POU) at the recruit depots. These "talking doctors" evaluate, report, advises, and sometime cause recruits to be separated from military service based on often unusual behavior or traits of some recruits, and many recruits are separated by POU early in the training. They had that power, and only the battalion commander could override their decisions. Back in the "day," since all recruits had sent their civilian clothing back home, if separated from service, they all got a blue suit of civilian clothing, and were sent home wearing Marine Corps underwear, shoes and socks with newly issued clothing consisting of blue trousers, shirt, and a coat or jacket. That practice, like "drumming out," has long since been stopped. Tom wanted Dynamite to be seen and evaluated by POU. I objected. I lost.

I had the duty that night. As a DI, you came in about 0530, worked until about 1730, and went home. But, every third day you had the duty. You remained from 0530 through the day and night, and through the next day until 1730. As usual, our poster boy corporal showed up at 0500 reveille, and Tom came in after breakfast about 0600. Dynamite had an appointment at POU at 0800. I told Tom I'd take Dynamite to POU for his appointment. This way I might be able to get in a positive statement about Dynamite. Perhaps sensing this, Tom told our poster boy to take Dynamite to POU. The two of them departed about 0730 as Tom and I began a daily training routine with the recruits. We drilled close order drill on the grinder (parade-deck) for an hour, had a classroom instruction for another hour or so, practiced the manual-of-arms, and went out for a three mile run before noon chow time. Tom said he'd take the platoon to chow, so, I walked back to the empty barracks to catch up on the five inch by eight inch index card file where we annotated remarks about specific recruits. It was like an informal fitness report system on all your recruits in your specific platoon.

I'd been in the DI House about half an hour when I heard footsteps in the hallway and heard the squadbay doors open and close. Curious, I went into the squadbay. Sitting on his footlocker, all alone in an empty squadbay, reading his guidebook, was private Dynamite. I was surprised. Very surprised!

"Private, what are you doing here?" I asked, as I approached. Dynamite jumped to the position of attention.

"Sir, the talking doctor told me to return to the barracks, Sir!"

"Then, you did go to POU with the corporal, didn't you?"

"Sir, yes Sir!"

"And, you did see the doctor?"

"Sir, yes Sir."

"What did he say?"

"Sir, he said for me to ease up a bit and quit being a "Sergeant Stryker (see *Sands of Iwo Jima*)." He said that all recruits had some weakness and if I didn't have any, I should invent one or two. He said this would take the "heat" off me. Sir!" Dynamite then looked directly at me. He knew he wasn't supposed to do that, but he did. For some reason, just in that instance, I let it slide. With a somewhat quivering, but strong voice, "I want to be a Marine, Sir!" He had tears welling in his eyes.

"Get your eyeballs off me, private!" I yelled at him.

He looked straight ahead and loudly repeated, "Sir! I want to be a Marine, Sir!!" Tears were running down his face.

I decided to change the conversation. "Private, where is your drill instructor, the corporal?"

"Sir, the doctor wanted to talk with him, Sir. That's when the doctor told me to return to my barracks. Sir."

"The doctor wanted to talk to the corporal?"

"Sir, yes Sir.'

"You walked back on your own?"

"Sir, yes Sir."

"Private, where is the corporal now?"

"Sir, this recruit does not know, Sir."

"What do you mean, you don't know?"

"Sir, I don't know because the talking doctors, well," he hesitated . . . "They kept him, Sir!"

I swear a subtle smile creased the lips of Dynamite as he spoke. Never saw the corporal again. Tom got a call from the Company Commander later in the afternoon. Tom never mentioned the phone call or the corporal. We received a sergeant to replace the corporal a couple of days later and we continued and completed the twelve week training cycle with our platoon.

Dynamite was our platoon's honor graduate from boot camp. Ironic, huh? I love it when I'm right. Occasionally!

Volunteers perform many duties and receive several benefits. They wear an issued uniform, and possess an identification card that allows them access into many South Carolina parks, exhibits, monuments, excursions, and places of interest free of charges. They receive quarterly information-filled lunches (real food) aboard *Yorktown*, travel to other museums and places of interest on an annual basis, and meet and greet some interesting individuals arriving and departing Patriots Point Naval and Maritime Museum. Many folks in the hierarchy here call them the backbone of this large organization.

If you are interested in becoming a volunteer or wish to make contributions to the Yorktown Foundation, step up! Walk in the steps of our heroes, and stand in their shadows with fellow volunteers. Become one of us, a Patriots Point Naval and Maritime Museum Volunteer.

It's a patriotic thing to do.

Ralph Stoney Bates, Sr.
Major USMC (Ret)
www.shortrations.com
Contributing Author and Executive Editor
Short Rations From Patriots Point Volunteers

AFTERWORD

There are countless museums dedicated to military history of the United States. The Naval and Maritime Museum at Patriots Point in South Carolina is one of them. It is a unique, one of them. The presence of the actual historic warships housing yet more historical artifacts, are themselves, alone, pieces of history. Within the same museum area is the recreated combat fire-support base derived from actual combat fire-support bases common during the war in Vietnam. Like the warships, within this replicated setting of a long-ago war, are other artifacts of that era. A command post, communications shacks, Southeast Asia barracks (hootch's), helicopters, vehicles, aide-station, and other buildings and implements of warfare are on display along with the discernable sounds of that time, in that place. The sounds of helicopters arriving and departing, vehicle engines whining, guns, large and small being fired, bird and animal sounds, even a navy river patrol boat sits idling in the water, are just some of the implements of that war that invade the senses, and stir the emotions of many of our visitors, and often recreating deep repressed memories of times past, but rarely forgotten. Yes, we are unique.

Most all military museums tend to educate the visitor of the significance of the surroundings within each of these museums. Toward that goal, supporting the museums are many dedicated staff members each with a vital role to play in presenting history in the best format possible. For most military museums, volunteers make up a significant part of that staff. These volunteers often tell a story from a personal experience outlining a piece of history sometimes known only to them. A personal story. A significant story. One that should be recorded for future generations. That is what inspired this anthology. **This is a recording of**

personal histories from the volunteers of this museum. And, a rendering of the museum as it exists today.

As time passes, one day there will be no survivors who served on the two warships, nor, will there be any survivors of the Vietnam War. Hopefully, this publication will survive to tell their stories, after they are gone.

The men and women volunteers of Patriots Point are unique. We have one who actually flew aircraft off the flight deck of the USS *Yorktown*. We have soldiers, sailors, airmen and Marines who served in the war in Vietnam. We have "tin-can" sailors, submariners, airmen, infantrymen, and pilots, telling and retelling their personal stories to countless visitors to our museum. We have career military, veterans, civilians, teachers, and others of all sorts of trades, occupations and experience. We have men and women, native born and immigrant, all volunteers who highlight the essence of our museum in their personal way. This anthology highlights not only our museum, but also the individual stories of those volunteers, often told in their own words. It was important that this be done. For, as one of the volunteers relayed to me, as he spoke of his background, "I'm telling this story of my experiences, not just for your book, but also for my grandchildren's grandchildren." So may it be.

This has been a presentment of *Short Rations From Patriots Point Volunteers.*

Ralph Stoney Bates, Sr., USMC (Ret)

Executive Editor/Author

Made in the USA
Monee, IL
09 January 2022

88571338R00134